To Mary

Best Wishes

Brian Thatcher

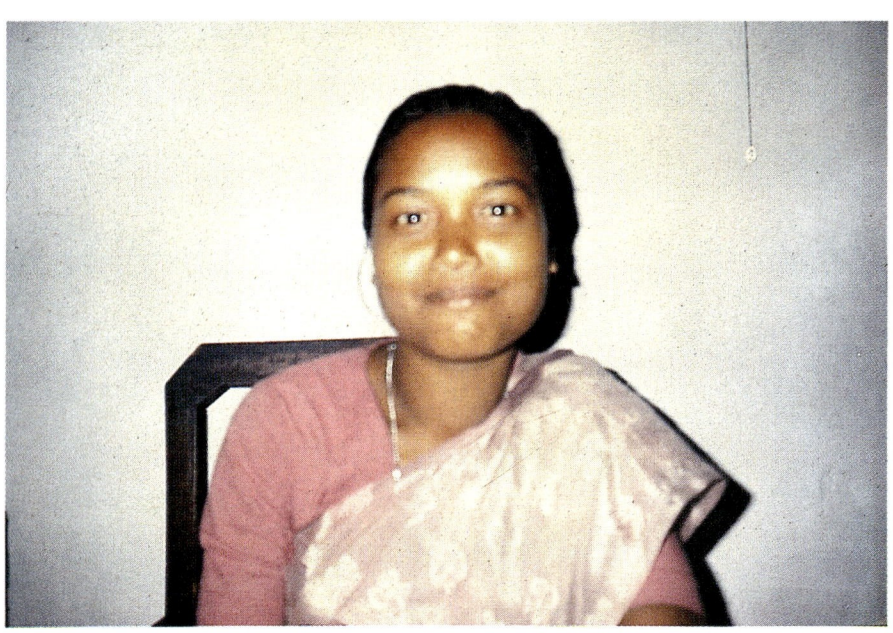

Albina Kujur, the reason the author went to India

COVER PHOTOGRAPHS
The Taj Mahal at Agra one of the seven wonders of the World. A friend's photogaph

Indian ladies, how fascinating is this Indian dancing. Albina third right with her friends

My Indian Journey

22 Days in the Sub-continent

by

Brian Holdich

First published in Great Britain in 1993 by
Brian's Books (B. W. Holdich),
4 Elm Close,
Market Deeping,
Peterborough.
PE6 8JN.

First published in 1993.
ISBN 0 9521017 0 X (Paperback)
My Indian Journey

British Library cataloguing-in-publication data. A
catalogue record for this book is available from the
British Library.

Printed and bound by Peter Spiegl & Co.,
6 St George's Street,
Stamford,
Lincolnshire.

I dedicate this book to my wife Kathleen, whose patience and understanding enabled me to visit India and to complete the story when I arrived home.

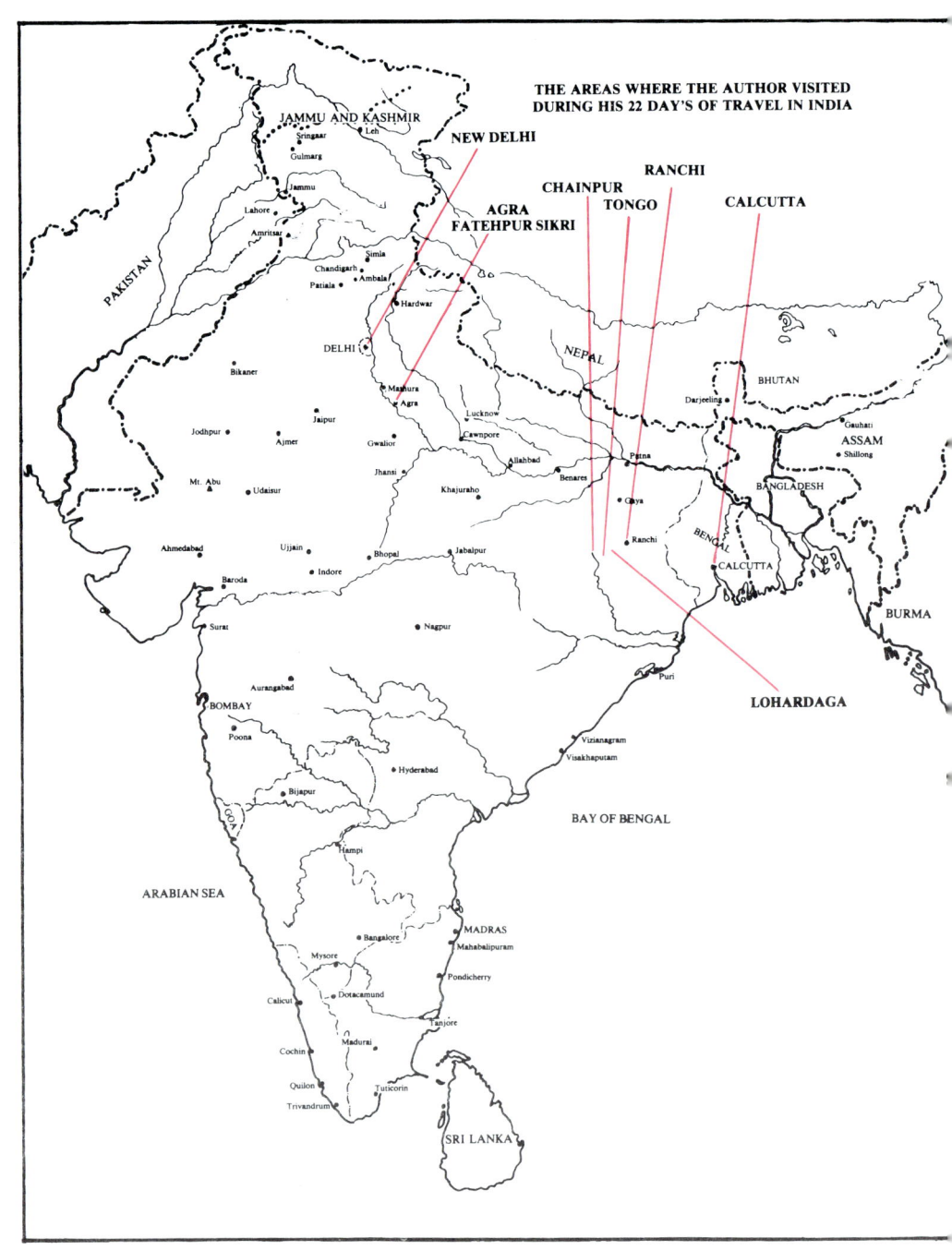

THE AREAS WHERE THE AUTHOR VISITED
DURING HIS 22 DAY'S OF TRAVEL IN INDIA

Contents

Acknowledgements

It is with immense gratitude that I give my thanks to the following people: To Dr John Heywood, who so kindly agreed to write the foreword to this book; I owe a great deal to Jan Dekker, whose patience was really tested by the constant changes made by me to my manuscript. He word processed everything I wrote many times; To David Morgan, who checked the proofs for spelling mistakes. Special thanks to Carol Biss, of the Book Guild Ltd. and R. Ross Stanton of the Janus Publishing Company for allowing me to put into print their thoughts on my book. I must acknowledge the great debt to Mother Teresa for granting me an audience with her and to MASU, co-workers of Mother Teresa, for sending me a photograph of her and giving me permission to use it in my book. I would like to thank the charity Action Aid, which works for children in the Third World. I was allowed to quote from any of its literature. Thanks, too, to my travel guides Sunny and Amin for their tours of New Delhi and Agra - what invaluable information I gained from them about India. Grateful I must be to my printers, Peter Spiegl & Co, of Stamford, for their helpfulness and meticulousness in the preparation and layout of this book. And finally, last but not least, thanks to the Ursuline sisters of Bihar, who gave me such valuable information about their lives and life in general in the Indian countryside.

Foreword

I have known Brian Holdich for more years than I dare to count. Our friendship began through our love of cricket and in the years that followed he has earned the respect of our community for the single-minded determination which he has shown with his fund raising activities for local charitable causes.

I was not surprised to learn that he had extended his care for others beyond the boundaries of Market Deeping, but those of us who know him were perhaps surprised to hear of his decision to visit India.

Brian's account of his journey is written in the same frank and straightforward style which is typical of him. It is always interesting and, in parts, very moving.

Knowing him as I do, I have no doubt that he will build his wall, just as I have no doubt that his journey to India broke down a wall that separated him from people in different countries. He found, in his journey, a common identity with those who he met and in writing this account of his experiences he gives us the opportunity to share that identity and to recognise the commonalty of mankind.

Dr. John Heywood,
Health Centre,
Market Deeping.

Introduction

"This is indeed India, the land that all men desire to see, and having seen once, by even a glimpse, would not give that glimpse for the shows of the rest of the world combined."

Mark Twain.

India. What an incredible and fascinating country it is. And what a vast country also - more than 900 million people live there. By the end of the century that figure could be well over 1,000 million. The population continues to grow in the largest democracy in the world. The British ruled this vast sub-continent, which before self-rule also included Pakistan and Bangladesh, from 1757 to independence in 1947. India dominates the south Asian sub-continent geographically and has borders with many countries, including Burma, Bangladesh, Pakistan, China, Nepal and Bhutan. Sri Lanka, a little island, lies off India's southern tip. India is a country with gigantic problems concerning the human race, these brought about by the sheer mass of people - the never-ending problem of a country bulging at the seams. The big cities of New Delhi and Calcutta are overflowing with millions. On a recent visit to this country I saw first-hand that India has just too many people. Every single day in India more than 70,000 babies are born. How can the country tackle this massive problem? Is there a solution? Is the answer as in China, where one child is allowed per married couple. Should birth control be used? I've asked myself this question many times since returning home to comfortable old England. I hope India finds the answer to this question. If not, then God only knows what will happen. India, being a Third World country, has enormous difficulties from being so very over-populated. A country just cannot keep producing thousands and thousands of babies every day like items being turned out off a conveyor belt. As the world approaches the 21st century, the problems concerning over-population in the Third World are of paramount importance. If these problems are not faced up to , millions will die. Walk through the slums of Calcutta like I have and you find that people really do simply lie down and die, usually from starvation.

The British Raj ruled India from the mid-17th century to 1947. Without British help I doubt whether India would have progressed through those years the way it has done. Having made that statement I'm sure that not everyone would agree with me. Mistakes were obviously made. I've recently spent 22 days in India and having spoken to many Indians, the majority were emphatic in asking "where would we be today" without the help the British were able to give. I was told that the British brought law and order to the country, along with magnificent buildings, roads, railways and cricket, and not necessarily in that order. Obviously the British Raj had a tremendous influence on the country. Go round any museum in India and the Raj stares down at one. The Raj may have left many years ago, but it is as though a ghost remains. It is like a smell, and believe me there are some dreadful smells in those big cities. And sometimes a smell doesn't go away too quickly, either. But to me it was as though the ghost of the British Raj just wouldn't go away. India is still very British and, looking at some of the old Victorian-style buildings, proud of it, too.

There is also a peculiar bond of affection between the British and Indian people, which I discovered repeatedly during my stay. There are many languages spoken in India, but English is often the second language to thousands. The majority of Indians can speak a limited amount of English without too much difficulty. Wherever I went on my travels through the country the majority of people could understand me, and I them. During recent holidays to Spain I always had great difficulty in making the Spanish understand me. Not so in India. The Raj brought this about. The Raj was very much the showpiece of the old British Empire. The Raj brought the game of cricket to this country. Cricket, being the national sport, is played and watched by millions. Here again there is an affection. Talk to any Indian about cricket and a barrier is immediately broken. In fact, so cricket-crazy is the average Indian that he will talk to you all day if you have the time - and Indians always seemed to have plenty of time. The Raj, therefore, departed from India many years ago, but the ghost remains and from that era there has sprung an association between two peoples which hopefully will never die.

The size of India is staggering. It covers an area of 3,287,263 square kilometres (1,268,884 square miles) - about twice the size of Alaska. To see it all one would need at least nine months of non-stop travel, and even then one could not possibly see it all. There are hundreds of religions, with over 80 per cent of the population Hindu. Eighty million Muslims live in India. Other religions include Christians, Jews, Sikhs, Jains, Buddhists and Parsis, with Hindi the most widely spoken language. India, as it moves forward, is gradually evolving into an industrial nation, progressing gradually in some areas and changing at an alarming speed in other parts of the country. The country area, which the normal tourist rarely sees, and where I was to spend nearly two weeks of blissfully happy days, ambles along in the same way it did centuries ago. Nothing here has changed and it could stay that way for a few more centuries still.

India is, in parts, a violent country, particularly in the north. Three leaders with the name of Gandhi have been assasinated, although Mahatma Gandhi was never Prime Minister. Terrorists in the far north are forever fighting the government. Terrible attrocities having taken place. Gangs of terrorists hold up trains, hundreds taken from railway carriages and shot. A lot of the troubles seem to be over the state of Kashmir, which is claimed by both India and Pakistan, and this area of conflict has been going on since 1947. Pakistan would like Kashmir to have its independence, but India says no.

The state of Bihar is said to be not only the most backward of all Indian states, but also the most violent and corrupt. This is where I would be spending the majority of my time during my 22-day stay in India. Here gangsters under the protection of politicians kill indiscriminately. Law and order, particularly in north Bihar, seems to have broken down. India certainly has many problems to solve. There is no doubt in my mind that the absolutely appalling poverty is caused by there simply being too many people. Yes, India has enormous problems. In a perfect world they would be solved, but life is not perfect as we all well know.

India, the country of maharajas and princes, of marbled palaces, of Rayput kingdoms, monuments, tombs, castles and forts. It is in parts exotic, mystical, extremely colourful, wild and enigmatic. It offers an impressive variety of history and culture. The mystery and beauty are there for all to see. The majestic hotels, where every whim will be yours. The sunset, particularly in the countryside, is not to be missed. There is a definite mystery about this land and I wanted to see it. This, then, was the country I wanted to see. I have been there and returned with a wealth of information I never had before. The experiences I had will remain with me for the rest of my life. Obviously in 22 days I only saw a very small part of a huge country. All my time was spent in the north of the country. What an education it has been. Because of my experiences I have a story to tell - a journey of over 5,000 miles to my final destination, which would take me through the big cities of New Delhi and Calcutta and the smaller ones of Agra and Ranchi. I would finally arrive in the south west tip of southern Bihar, where I had the feeling I had arrived at the back of beyond.

My trip would take me to see the towering spectacular Taj Mahal, the monument to an emperor's undying love; to see the unbelievable and indescribable poverty in the cities; to delve into the history of the Black Hole of Calcutta; to see the magnificent Eden Gardens cricket ground; to meet, of all people, Mother Teresa, one of the truly great human beings of the world, who lives in the slums of Calcutta. And in those slums I was to see some of the most strikingly beautiful women and children I have ever seen - and these poor people were just beggars on the streets. I wouldn't have missed my trip to India for anything, so because of my experiences I've decided to write this book. Calcutta held a strange attraction for me. I feared the worst. Instead, amongst the squalor I found an extremely friendly people. I was actually to grow very fond of the place, and in many respects I felt sad to leave it. There is a buzz about this city. I felt a tingling excitement every time I walked shoulder to shoulder through its streets of millions of people, and, apart from one incident when I thought my life was in danger, I felt perfectly safe. I would put on my walking boots and walk many miles, this, I decided, being the best way to see Calcutta. Walking through those terrible slums I found many smiling faces. It has been said that Calcutta has a soul. Well, I've seen that soul. It is certainly a city I could visit again. Calcutta was to me a big surprise, and a nice one at that.

When I was to arrive at my final destination in south west Bihar I was to be welcomed by the Ursuline sisters of Bihar. I was to travel and stay at different convent schools in this area. I was to be taken into the near-secret world of their lives. How well they looked after me. I shall always remember them with great affection. I lived with them for nearly two weeks. Any fears I may have had about living in a convent school quickly receded. I spent the majority of my stay at the Ursuline Convent School in the village of Tongo, where I was to live with 16 Ursuline sisters. I jokingly called them the Divine Sisters of Tongo. Their love of God was something I'd never seen before. These brides of Christ became the best friends any man could wish to have. Nothing was ever too much trouble for them in their willingness to look after me. Their wicked sense of humour was certainly something I didn't expect to find in a convent school. I am indeed proud to call each and every one of them my friend and I shall never forget them.

The main purpose of my trip, however, was finally to meet Albina Kujur, a young lady whom I'd sponsored through the charity Action Aid, so she could attend the Ursuline Convent School at Tongo. I had written to her and she to me over a period of ten years. When she left school I lost contact with her for three years. But thankfully I was able to make contact with her again. So, on having "re-found" her I decided, at the invitation of Sister Bernadette Tete, the senior school headmistress, to visit her. This invitation was too good an opportunity for me to miss. I therefore made up my mind to visit my sponsored child that was. When we finally met at Ranchi Airport I was struck by her beauty and her disposition. She was a young lady of 24 years. She knew what she wanted in her life and that was to be a school teacher, which, considering her humble background, was quite an ambition. She is, at present, at Lohardaga Ursuline Training College in Bihar training to be a teacher. Nobody, I can assure you, will be more proud of her than me when she passes those exams.

I was to spend a truly unforgettable day with her family, who gave me a hero's welcome to their humble home. By travelling to southern Bihar I was to finish up in the Indian countryside that the tourist rarely sees. I was to visit deepest India, Mahatma Gandhi's India. He had this vision that the real India lay in the country areas. The countryside in the Tongo area was absolutely beautiful. I'd never before seen such colouring in a countryside. This, then, was the countryside where Albina Kujur was born, born to a tribal people called Oron, who settled in this area many centuries ago. I was to find such love, happiness and contentment in her home. Has the Western world got it right, I've often asked myself since I arrived home. There is no greed or selfishness there like one can find in the Western world. These were basically a happy people, a desperately poor people, who, I thought, had their priorities right. They are also a very religious people. To me they were the beautiful people of India. I've been to Gandhi's India alright. These people from the tribe of Oron are the original rat eaters of India, known for this because it was at one time their only hope of survival. In this book you will read of me thinking that when I visited them on that memorable day I was in fact eating rats meat. If it was rats meat I'll never know, but if it was good enough for those tribal people it was good enough for me. I ate it and was none the worse for it.

So this is my story, an unusual travel story. What I have written of is, of course, only a small part of my journey through India, but I do honestly believe I have a story to tell. Before I left England I was determined to write down everything that happened on my journey. I would have a diary every day, starting at day one on November 8, when I left England, to day 22 - November 29 - when I returned. Every day I would write down the day's events. On some days I would write down events as they actually happened, sometimes while in an aircraft. You will also learn of my fear of flying. I went through agonies at times. This book will be an honest book and I hope a sincere one. If I am critical at times it's because I found what I saw to be so unjust. The poverty I'll never forget. The caste system in India, where people are born into different social classes, I found unfair. Life is not always fair in this world and in India a lot of what I saw seemed most unfair. As you read through my experiences in My Indian Journey I might even make you laugh - of that I'm sure - and hopefully not make you cry. This is my first venture into book writing. I've already said that this will be an honest book. Perhaps some of my honesty will shock you, but it would serve no purpose if I was less than honest. Much of what I've written reflects what I felt at the time. And since I've been home in England getting the book down on paper I've felt little need to change what I wrote of a particular day's events.

After much deliberation I've decided that the title of my book will be My Indian Journey, which seemed the most appropriate title. Whether it sells or not only time will tell, but my dearest wish is that the book will sell enough copies for me to help financially towards the repairs to the compound wall that circles the Ursuline Convent School in Tongo. This wall needs repairing if only to keep out thieves who are forever stealing from the convent. This, then, is my main reason for writing the book.

Having been home in England now for many months, my desire now is to give something back to those wonderful Ursuline sisters, the brides of Christ who were absolute angels to me.

So come with me now on My Indian Journey, the journey being the realisation of a dream to meet at last a poor Indian girl called Albina Kujur. We met through sponsorship and if I'd never sponsored her I certainly would never have met her. I can truthfully say that sponsorship works. I've seen it at first hand. Millions of children are crying out for sponsorship in the Third World. Helping a child in the Third World was my way of helping someone who was less fortunate than myself. Giving a child an education through sponsorship is the finest way one can help these unfortunate children, who didn't ask to be born into such poverty-stricken countries. Education is the greatest gift we can give to the Third World. Without education one is nothing and ignorance prevails.

So this is my story and I only hope that people who read this book will not accuse me of being vain. Believe me, vanity doesn't come into it. I realise the book is mostly about me. But I can assure you that my main purpose in writing it is to help repair that wall, and I genuinely think I have interesting story to tell. But before starting at day one, please read about the Ursuline sisters and Action Aid sponsorship. I hope you enjoy reading about my journey as much as I have enjoyed writing about it, and maybe, just maybe, someone somewhere will sponsor a child in the Third World through a charity like Action Aid. And if just one person does that My Indian Journey will have been well worthwhile.

The Ursuline Convents And Sponsorship

In 1978 I sponsored a young girl called Albina Kujur so that she could attend the Ursuline Convent School for Girls in the village of Tongo in the state of Bihar in India. I sponsored her through the charity Action Aid. Action Aid works with children, families and communities to improve the quality of life in some of the poorest parts of the world. I was to pay a small monthly sum of money to Action Aid so that this girl could have an education which, otherwise, she might not have had. She was born into extreme poverty. Her parents were so poor they found it difficult to provide adequate food and clothing for her. They also had five other children. Albina was born into a family of peasant farmers. They could only allow their children to have two frugal meals a day and because of this the children were undernourished. Through taking out this sponsorship for her I felt I was helping a child in the Third World, so that, hopefully, she could make something of herself which only education can bring - and escape the appalling poverty she was born into.

When I wrote to Action Aid in 1978 concerning sponsorship I was sent a photograph of Albina, who was eleven years old. I was struck by the sheer helplessness of the child's face. Her face had a "please help me" look about it. I knew I couldn't refuse that face. Yes, she was to be my sponsored child and I felt good inside about it. I was told that a personal relationship could emerge between the sponsor and the child. Action Aid also sent me a case history of Albina, generally informing me of her life to date in India. She was also to have a case number, which was always to be used when I wrote letters to her. Action Aid also informed me that she would have the happiness and security that stems from the knowledge that someone cares enough to give her food to eat and clothes to wear and wants her to benefit from having an education. I was told that I was giving a child a chance in the Third World. If I would sponsor her, her miserable life could only get better.

I was to sponsor Albina Kujur from 1978 to 1988. She attended the convent school in Tongo as a day student. During those years we would write to each other three or four times a year. Her letters were always full of interest. Usually she would write about her school work and also about her family, and generally about her life in the Indian countryside. She would write to me in Hindi, which was translated by her into English. Also, at the bottom of each letter was a school report from her teacher. Her ambition from quite early in life was to go to college. This was very ambitious of her. Here, I thought, was no ordinary girl. As the years went by my ambition was to visit India and meet her. That personal relationship that Action Aid had spoken about was to me very real indeed. I wanted to see for myself what sort of girl she was. I wanted to visit the Ursuline Convent School in Tongo. This, then, was my ambition.

In 1988 Albina's letters suddenly stopped. A year went by and I heard nothing. Then Action Aid wrote to me saying that Albina had been taken out of the school sponsorship programme. She had left the Tongo school and would hopefully find herself work, and would I sponsor another child. I agreed to sponsor another child, but I wrote back to Action Aid asking if I could help Albina in any way, as I knew she wished to go to college. After ten years of correspondence I felt somehow responsible for her. Action Aid wrote back saying they couldn't be responsible for a girl who was not in the school sponsorship programme anymore. As all my previous letters over the past ten years had been addressed to the Tongo convent school I decided to write there again. Twice I Wrote, but never did I receive a reply. As I never knew Albina's home address, and she didn't know mine, my chances of meeting her were now, therefore, very slim. She could have moved to anywhere in India to find work. It looked as if I'd lost her. I would now never meet her, or so it seemed.

During the Christmas holiday period of 1990 I was cleaning up my office desk when I came upon all the letters that Albina Kujur had sent to me over the ten-year period. I began to read them all again. What would she be doing now, I thought. She could be married with children. I would just have liked to know, though, if she was well and where she was. I decided, therefore, to write once again to the Ursuline Convent School, Tongo. Could you tell me, I wrote, what has happened to Albina Kujur. Please tell me if she is well and what she is doing. I also gave the school Albina's case number. I posted the letter to the headmistress of Tongo school and waited for a reply. I did not, in fact, hold out much hope of one. The two previous letters I had written nearly two years ago had not yielded a reply, but I hoped this time it would be different.

In March 1991 a letter from the Ursuline Convent School, Tongo, came in my post. This was the reply I'd been waiting for. The letter was from Sister Bernadette Tete, the headmistress of the school, saying that she had received my letter and that she was pleased to inform me that Albina Kujur was very much alive and well. She was studying to be a primary school teacher at Chainpur College, which was only a few miles from Tongo. Also, Sister Bernadette had said that if I wanted to visit India she would be only too pleased to let me stay at the Tongo convent school. So I decided within days of receiving the letter to accept Sister

Bernadette's kind invitation. I was on my way to India at last. I would finally meet Albina Kujur.

After writing to Sister Bernadette of my intention to come to India on November 8, 1991 - I would be away from England for 22 days - I arranged my itinerary with an Indian travel company. While I was in India for those 22 days I intended to see as much of the country as possible. I arranged to visit New Delhi, Agra, Calcutta, Ranchi and finally southern Bihar, where I would be spending the majority of my time. In June 1991 I received another letter from India, this time from Albina. In this letter she told me there had been some disturbances at Chainpur College, strike troubles, I believe, and that the college had closed down until further notice. She also said how excited she was about my coming to India, that she couldn't wait to meet me and that she was counting the days. I then received another letter from Sister Bernadette saying that Albina had got a place at Lohardaga Ursuline Convent Training College to continue her studies to be a primary school teacher. Lohardaga was about 30 miles from Tongo and she would be living-in there. The course was for two years and Albina was thrilled about these new developments. She had been extremely fortunate to get a place at this college. Also, the good news was that she would be able to have a week off college to be with me. This was great news, I thought. Also, Sister Bernadette and Albina would be at Ranchi airport to meet me on Novermber 15, when I would be flying in from Calcutta. I couldn't believe my luck. I really was nearly on that aircraft to New Delhi. India beckoned, and I couldn't wait.

The Ursuline convent schools for girls are spread throughout the state of Bihar. The Ursuline sisters of Tildonk first came to India in 1903. Four Belgian sisters opened a convent school in Ranchi. Soon other convent schools were opened, the Tongo school being opened in 1907.

From these small beginnings, the number of convent schools grew to the present total of 24. A total of 500 sisters live and teach at these convent schools. The Congregation of the Ursuline Sisters of Tildonk was founded by the Reverend John Lambertz on April 30, 1818, and under his guidance and inspiration a school for children was opened in Tildonk. Soon, women as devoted as him worked together in the education of the parish, this being known as the Presbytery. As the Presbytery increased its number of sisters and more children attended the school, it was soon evident that the Presbytery was not big enough. So work was started on the site where the Ursuline convent stands today. By 1832 the institute was recognised as a religious congregation and many sisters pronounced their final vows in the presence of an archbishop.

When Father Lambertz died in 1869 the congregation numbered 43 convents and by now they had opened in Holland and England. India (1903), Canada (1914) and America (1924) followed. In 1978 a General Government was formed with authority for the overall government of the congregation. For the first time in its history the congregation of Tildonk had an international government, and in 1982 the Ursuline Congregation of Tildonk was granted pontifical status by the Holy See. From the humble beginnings established by Father Lambertz the congregation is today based in many parts of the world. He would indeed be a very proud man if he could see how it has grown worldwide.

When the four original white Belgian sisters came to Ranchi in 1903 they had the problem of persuading parents to allow their children to attend the school. Indian parents in those early days were very sceptical about allowing their children to go to school. Education was something they knew nothing about. Besides, many of the children were wanted by their parents for work and, particularly in the country areas, for work in the fields. Today, in some cases, the Ursuline sisters still visit families in Bihar to persuade parents to send their children to school. In the Tongo school, where I was to spend the majority of my time, there are 1,300 schoolchildren. Generally, parents now realise the value of an education and are only too pleased that their children are getting one. Without these Ursuline convent schools thousands of Indian children would not be getting an education, as 40 per cent of all Indian children go without any schooling.

The Ursuline Sisters of Tildonk work in many parts of the world today, often in very dangerous areas. Some go to many countries where they feel they are best suited to help God. They have given their lives to Him. I now quote from three extracts from Fullness in the Life of Christ, from the General Constitutions of the Ursuline Sisters of the Congregation of Tildonk. To my mind these three extracts will, hopefully, explain a sister's devotion to God.

"You are His, you belong to Him. You have offered yourselves to Him with generosity and with your whole being He has accepted you."

(Letter to London 1852, Father John Lambertz).

"They should give honour to Jesus Christ, to whom they have vowed their virginity and their entire selves. They must place their love and trust in God alone."

(5th Counsel of St Angela Merici).

"My whole life will forever reflect the greatness of my Lord, my whole person lies open to God, my saviour, expanding with grateful joy, while with unhoped-for tenderness he has favoured this response of his willing maid."

(Mary's Magnificat, Luke 1.46.48).

In November 1991 I was privileged to visit the Ursuline Convent School for Girls in the village of Tongo in southern Bihar. I was to meet 16 Ursuline sisters who are carrying on the good work the four original sisters from Belgium started in Bihar in 1907. All these sisters are school teachers and they are giving the children of this very backward area of India an education which they undoubtedly would not otherwise have received. Because I'm so proud to have met them, because of their wonderful hospitality to me and because they feature so prominently in this book I now list each and every one of them. They have made the supreme sacrifice of giving their lives to God. I salute these sisters of the Order of St Ursula (OSU):

Sister Albina Dungoung
Sister Josephine Ekka
Sister Bernadette Tete
Sister Michael Turkey
Sister Alphonsa Vadasari
Sister Vianney Chadathi
Sister Fredric Lomga
Sister Teresita Panna
Sister Arrivita Coppa
Sister Scholastica Miry
Sister Anna Kerketta
Sister Angela Coppa
Sister Sushila Ekka

Sister Goretti Lakra
Sister Arririt Kerketta
Sister Maxima Bara   (all OSU)

When I first wrote to Action Aid in 1978 about sponsorship of a child in India I was sent a rather chilling letter about where my sponsored child was living. This letter probably gives a fair indication of what life is like in the countryside of Bihar today. Over the ten-year period of sponsoring Albina I regularly used to read this letter and I often wondered what on earth life was really like there. The more I read this letter the more curious I became. Was it really as bad as the letter said? Evidently the people of this area lived in an "on-going cycle of misery" from which they were "unable to escape". The area certainly seemed to be off the beaten track. Through my curiosity, the ambition arose to visit the area. So on November 7 1991 my suitcases were packed and I was ready for a great adventure, all last-minute details tied up. On November 8 My Indian Journey would begin and I would record the events of each day, sometimes as they actually happened. I felt I was going to the back of beyond. I was going to an area of India that the tourist would rarely see. The letter from Action Aid read as follows"

"Bihar, India.

"Bihar is a relatively small state in the north east of India, approximately 200 miles from Calcutta. It is one of the poorest and most densely populated areas in the world. Due to the extremely deprived conditions under which many of the people live it is an area which in recent years has experienced considerable political unrest. For most of the people living in remote, isolated areas the agitations have passed unnoticed. They live in an on-going cycle of misery from which they are unable to escape. Poverty breeds ignorance, which in turn breeds ill-health, leading to un-productive farming.

"The land on which these people must rely is exhausted. There is no money to buy chemical fertilizer and animal manure must be dried and burned as fuel. Wells for irrigation are expensive and rare. The peasant farmers must rely on erratic rains, which for the past years have come too early, too late or not at all.

"Action Aid, working in co-operation with the Ursuline Sisters of Bihar, have taken responsibility for 2,000 children whose families are unable to properly feed, clothe and educate them. Most of the families are from Aboriginal tribes. They are the people who populated India in the years before the Hindu invasions many centuries BC. The Hindus call these people "rat eaters" because many of them are so poor that they have been forced to survive in this manner.

"Illiteracy is common, malnutrition is universal, disease and early death are everyday facts of life. In the years to come Action Aid hopes to expand its activities and begin vocational training programmes to create job opportunities so that these children will one day be able to support themselves and their families. Their children in turn will never again need the help of a sponsorship programme."

So, on the eve of my flight to India I was raring to go. This was to be the journey of a lifetime. It proved to be the most momentous and exhilirating 22 days of my life. Just about every day was incident-packed from start to finish. On November 7 I was buzzing with excitement. Here I was, a newly-acquired 56-year-old grandfather acting like an excitable schoolboy. I went to bed that evening hardly expecting to sleep. I really was so very hyped up. So much was going through my mind. I'd wanted to make this trip for years. I was finally going to make it, a dream come true, as it were. As I lay in bed that last night at home I wondered what on earth the next three weeks would offer - what was India really like? I couldn't wait for the alarm clock to go off at 4.30am the next morning. So come with me now, the big aircraft is waiting at Gatwick Airport to jet me off to New Delhi. Get ready to fasten your seatbelts - my adventure through India will start the very second that alarm clock goes off. India calls, My Indian Journey was about to begin, and I just couldn't wait to jump out of bed in the early hours of Friday, November 8, 1991.

Day One 8.11.91

Market Deeping To New Delhi

The alarm went off at 4.30. "This is it," I said, as I jumped out of bed.

"I've had a terrible night's sleep," Kathleen said. "Well, I've hardly slept at all," I remarked. My wife then told me it was 4.15am and not 4.30am. I can never set alarm clocks right, I thought.

But enough of this small talk. I was off on a great adventure. I had been waiting for this day for nearly nine months. I was off to the Indian sub-continent finally to see a certain somebody I'd been hoping to meet for years. I had made contact again with my sponsored child Albina Kujur, who was not a child anymore but 24 years old and a student at a teacher training college in Lohardaga in the state of Bihar in north east India. I had wanted to meet her since we first exchanged letters when she was just eleven years old. I was on my way at last.

In March of this year I had made up my mind to travel to India to see her and a date of November 8 had been set for my departure. The summer months had been long, yet the last few weeks had flown by. The excitement increased in the last few days. But I was also getting nervous as to what she would think of me, or what I would think of her. We were finally going to meet. I just hoped that neither of us would be disappointed.

I was also getting apprehensive about my flight. I do not relish the thought of flying at all. I have a genuine fear of flying. Only those people who have this fear like me will know what I mean. If God had wanted us to fly he would have supplied us with wings, I thought.

Here I was setting off on a journey of nearly 11,000 miles, this being the distance from England to India and back. I would be up in the sky for nearly 24 hours with five different flights to catch. Crazy, isn't it? I must be mad, I thought, as I said my goodbyes to my wife and son, who had driven me down to Gatwick Airport from my home in Market Deeping, Lincolnshire. I didn't want to upset my wife, but she knew the way I was feeling, and she also knew that at that particular moment I would have given anything not to be boarding that British Airways flight No. B035. I hate goodbyes because they can be forever and when I saw that big hunk of metal waiting to take off I thought what many thousands of other people had thought: How on earth is that aircraft going to get off the ground?.

On the car journey to Gatwick I had been unusually quiet. It had rained - something else I had to worry about. Would flight B035 be able to take off with puddles of water on the runway? This fear of flying had really got inside me to the point where I thought I would never see my family again. Puddles on the runway would cause the aircraft to not quite lift itself from the ground at the appropriate time. I was looking for all sorts of excuses for the 'plane to crash. I was putting myself through absolute hell. I was deeply sorry I'd upset my wife, and upset her I had. I should have hidden my feelings better. Anyone would have thought I was leaving her for far more than just 22 days. I suppose after 30 years of marriage even being away from my family for just three weeks would seem a long time. After all, I do believe that in that 30-year period my wife had only been away from me for a week at the most, usually when she went to visit her parents. But this was a flight I just had to make. I wanted to meet Albina Kujur, and if it meant the only way I could see her was to fly thousands of miles in an aircraft, then there was no alternative - this was a journey I had to make.

I am writing these first pages of my diary on board the 'plane. It has been airborne one and a half hours. The flight seems normal. It had left Gatwick 20 minutes late. Now I've got feelings of guilt. Had I been selfish in taking this flight to see a young lady whom I'd never met? I had put my own interests first. Had I really taken my wife's considerations into account when I so casually informed her I was going to India and that I would be away for 22 days? What sort of person was I to leave my wife at home worrying herself sick while I flew thousands of miles in pursuit of a dream? Was I really that selfish? I had the best wife in the world. Not many men would have got away with it. Yes, I felt guilty. I should have considered my wife more. I really had been very selfish.

When we sat down to talk of my intentions to visit India we had talked at length and we had decided, or was it I, that although my wife would love to see the Taj Mahal and that although I would be staying at excellent hotels in New Delhi and Calcutta, we had no idea what the standard of accommodation would be in Ranchi. And also, for nearly two weeks in the latter part of my holiday, I would be staying in the area of southern Bihar, and although I'd had this offer to stay as long as I wanted in the convent schools in the area, what say if one week was quite long enough? What then? I was, after all, going into unknown territory. I'd never stayed at a convent before. A week could be quite long enough, and if we did move on from there, where would we move to? I dreaded to think what the standard of hotels was like in the country areas of India. So we both decided that it would be better if my wife didn't come. There were just too many unanswered questions, so the decision was made that I would go on my own. If then the going got tough I would have only myself to think about.

The flight is now three hours old. I'm pleased to say there is very little turbulence. The elderly Indian gentleman at the side of me has dropped off to sleep like he said he would. He tells me that he has been visiting relations in Leicester. His wife sits at the other side of him near the window. I have been giving him my brandy, which of course is free. His wife has also been giving him her brandy. "I like brandy," he says. He must have drunk at least ten small bottles of it. He informs me that yesterday in Leicester he was drinking all day. I believed him, too. To see him drinking his brandy, he was obviously a heavy drinker. When I told him we were flying over Austria he kept saying Australia. He was well gone and in a very deep sleep, at peace with the world, I thought. I smile to myself, "I like brandy," he says.

Having departed from Gatwick at 11am I look at my watch and it's 5pm, about 11pm Indian time. I have watched the new Robin Hood film with Kevin Costner - it certainly passes the time on a long flight. It was an excellent film. I'm sure the Robin Hood story will never die. It will soon be teatime. The lunch we had at 1pm was just right - not too heavy. It was English food, thank goodness. Thinking about Indian food, with all its spices, curries and rice etc I do not know how on earth I shall manage. I've got to be honest, I do not like Indian food. I am very much a roast beef and Yorkshire pudding man. I could eat Yorkshire pudding every day. I know I can be a bore where food is concerned. If my wife and I ever go out for dinner, Yorkshire pudding has to be on the menu. I'm really beginning to wonder how I shall manage Indian food. There's one thing for sure, I shall not starve. Indian food will have to be eaten. If one is hungry, one eats, whatever it is.

There are about 300 people on board. A good half are Indians. I'm struck by the many colours of the saris these Indian women wear - how dazzlingly colourful they are. I'm sure these people are of the upper caste of Indian society. The children look so clean and well dressed and the man of the family certainly looks the prosperous type. I've read so much about the caste system of India recently that I wonder if I shall come across it in my travels. I think of Albina - her upbringing would be so different to that of these people. Her family would be of the lower caste of Indian society. I'm sure I shall see the caste system at work in the next three weeks. I must admit, though, that from what I've read it seems most unfair.

I am writing now in my room at the Hotel Oberoi Maidens, New Delhi. The 'plane touched down at New Delhi International Airport at 6.55pm. The flight took seven hours, 55 minutes. A perfect flight. I was so relieved when the 'plane got down that I wanted to go to the cockpit and shake the captain by the hand. I get through customs without any trouble and manage to change some travellers cheques for India currency. I am met at the airport by a representative of the travel company I booked my holiday with, all very efficient. Nothing is too much trouble for this man. His name is Kev and we make our way through the masses of people and traffic to where his car is. He introduces me to the driver and we are off. I take my first look at India. It's dark, but even in the darkness I can see appalling squalor.

On the half-hour drive to the hotel Kev talks about cricket. "Do you like cricket?" he asks. Here I am sitting in this car and one of the first people I talk to on arriving here asks me if I like cricket. I would like this man to have asked my wife if her husband likes cricket. If she had been with me she would have said that it is because her husband is cricket mad that she has become a cricket widow. Kev informed me that South Africa were in India for three one-day internationals. He told me that interest in these matches was at fever pitch. I knew India was a cricket-mad country. It felt good to be here and I knew I was going to enjoy my stay.

Kev wanted to know what my occupation was. I work for the Prudential Assurance Company Ltd, I said, at this point feeling quite proud of my company. "Never heard of them," he says. "I've heard of lots of life assurance companies, but never the Prudential." I Felt slightly dejected. I thought Prudential Assurance was known the world over. I would have to educate this man. He dropped me off at the hotel and I'm writing this now while sitting up in bed. I've had to move my watch on six hours to Indian time. I think of home. The time would be nine o'clock. If I were there now I would be getting ready for my Friday evening game of snooker at Market Deeping Snooker Club. So here I am on Indian soil. The hotel is magnificent, quite one of the best I've been in. I'm very tired now and I'll close this Day One of the diary.

Day Two 9.11.91

New and Old Delhi

I awoke at 8.15 am after finally getting to bed last night at 3.30am. I go down to breakfast at 9am, an English breakfast I might add. At the table I am reading the morning paper, The Times of India, English-printed. The front page is full of bombings, murders etc. Here, then, is just a part of the news on November 9 in New Delhi, India.

Quake Rocks Capital, it says. On November 8 (PTI), an earthquake measuring 6.3 on the Richter Scale rocked the capital at 8.44pm, causing people to flee their houses in panic. The paper goes on to mention that in Varnasi five people were killed and others seriously injured as a result of communal violence. At least seven people killed in a bomb blast in a train as the train was nearing Kalyan Station. At least 20 people injured.

Also to catch my eye - In Bihar, which is my final destination, at least 25 people killed when a bus fell into a ditch and 50 others quite seriously injured. The accident happened as the driver lost control of the speeding and overloaded bus. Also on November 8, a Soviet 'plane crashes into mountains, killing all 38 people on board. That will do my confidence the world of good, as in two days time I fly to Calcutta.

On reading this newspaper I realise that I am now in a violent country. As I read through it countless murders are being committed all over India. The earthquake situation can be quite worrying - after all it was only three weeks ago that more than 1,000 were killed when an earthquake struck in northern India, which is only a few hundred miles away from here. The state of Kashmir seems to be continually in the news, only here in New Delhi it is more so. With New Delhi, of course, being in the north of the country, India can rightly claim that this state belongs to her. Pakistan thinks differently and would like Kashmir to have its independence. These two countries have certainly had their differences over the years. It makes me wonder whether India and Pakistan can ever live in peaceful harmony like other parts of the world. In England, of course, we have the Northern Ireland problem. Will these problems ever be solved? Will this world of ours ever be a completely trouble-free world? I would like to think it would be, but I doubt it. But we must have hope.

After breakfast my guide for the day introduces himself to me in the hotel foyer. His name is Sunny. Today I am to have a tour of New Delhi and also Old Delhi. I'm really looking forward to this guided tour. Outside the hotel I'm introduced to the driver, Mr Singh. The car is an old-style Morris Ambassador.

This huge city is divided into two parts, New and Old. New Delhi is India's capital, and like all Indian cities it grows at an alarming pace. It is the gateway to India and has a population of more than seven million people. Sunny turned out to be an excellent guide. He was a real education and an Indian character through and through. He seemed to know every inch of Delhi. Delhi is, of course, an historic city, quite elegant in parts. The thronged bazaars and Moghul architecture of Old Delhi contrast with the formal splendour of New Delhi. Sunny knew what he was doing, he was an experienced guide and I would benefit from this.

The Government buildings, the circular Parliament, the National Museum, Shah Janan's imposing citadel, the Red Fort built at the eastern extreme of the walled city and the Mahatma Gandhi memorial are just a few of the memories I shall take home with me.

Talking again about my guide Sunny, he took me everywhere. A good guide can light up a place before your very eyes. A poor guide is just the opposite. Sunny was making my stay in Delhi full of interest and I was indeed very grateful.

Today I have seen what poverty is. I have seen it through these tourist's eyes. What I have seen today may even haunt me for years to come. We had hardly got through the hotel gates this morning when our car pulled up at traffic lights. Looking out of the window at the appalling squalor of this city I spotted a young girl of about seven years of age risking serious injury as she began dodging the traffic on this very busy road in her haste to get to our car to clean the windscreen, hoping, of course, that Sunny would give her a Rupee. Sunny told her to go away. She pleaded with him to give her some money - a Rupee is about equivalent to two pence in English money. Again he said no. Then she saw me in the back seat. She scratched with her fingernails at the side window. There was a look of terror in her eyes. She looked terribly thin, quite ill and dirty. I saw fear of a kind I hadn't seen before. She made me feel ill just looking at her. I went to my pocket to give her a ten Rupee note. As I opened the window she snatched it from my hand, and she was gone. I shall see that pathetic little face long after I've arrived home in England. Her matchstick figure I'll never forget. She was so thin that a mild breeze would have blown her over.

I talked to Sunny of this incident. He said I shouldn't have given her money. The car pulled away from the traffic lights and what followed was degradation such as I hadn't seen before. I saw poverty that I'd only read about in the newspapers or seen on TV in England. This was indeed new to me, and somewhat frightening. The look on people's faces, particularly the children, will definitely haunt me this Christmas. Everybody looked so undernourished. So this is what hell is like, I thought - children crying in the streets of Delhi for want of a good meal. Sunny then said something that surprised me. He said there were not really any poor beggars in Delhi. "Now take Calcutta," he said, "that's where you will find the really poor beggars." To me a beggar is a beggar wherever he may be. I then thought to myself 'could Calcutta really be worse than this?'. If it is, then I'm not sure I can face it.

Delhi is a noisy city. On every street corner loudspeakers seem to blaring out music. Every car, lorry and bus blasts its horn. The masses of people in their thousands cram the streets, people are crammed like sardines into buses, with more on the roofs and half a dozen or so hanging onto the passenger door, one foot inside and the other dangling outside. Pedal cycle rickshaws, scooter rickshaws and motorcycle rickshaws are to be seen by the thousand. I even saw four people on one motorcycle. They couldn't have done it better if it had been a stage show somewhere. Young mothers holding babies barely a month old in their arms, sitting on the pillion seat of a motorcycle with not one arm around the waist of the driver or holding onto anything, but seemingly balancing themselves on the pillion seat while the driver of the motorcycle dodges in and out of the traffic. How the young mother and her baby didn't fall off I'll never know. Mr Singh, our driver, proved to be exceptionally good, which I think one has to be to drive on such crowded roads. Sunny remarked that to be a good driver in Delhi one needs a good head, a good pair of hands and good luck.

Sunny seemed to know a lot about Indian politics. He works for the Indian tourist board. When he was at college his great ambition was to be Prime Minister of India. I quickly looked at him thinking he was joking - he wasn't, he was deadly serious. He must have had many disappointments along the way. He spoke of total disillusionment with politics in India. The Muslims, he says, are forever blowing up people in the north. Terrorists are in Delhi and mixing with ordinary people. These terrorists, he said, would turn up on a person's doorstep in the middle of the night and demand a bed and meal. If the poor person who opened the door refused to co-operate he was shot dead there and then. Also, the screams of young girls can be heard as they are being raped, and certainly not getting any mercy from the rapist.

"Politicians are just a bunch of bananas," Sunny says. "When they arrive in Parliament they are green, then they become yellow and not one of them is straight. And if they stay too long they become rotten."

At this point we were travelling past the circular Parliament building when he said: "Why is the Indian Parliament round in shape?" I confessed I didn't know. "Because you can't corner the so-and-so politicians," he said.

Sunny then suggested I should see the world famous Indian carpets. At the time we were right in the busy Delhi shopping area. We hopped out of the car while Mr Singh drove off elsewhere. We would see him again, Sunny said, in three hours. We walked into this carpet shop, I was introduced to the owner and Sunny disappeared to wait for me outside. A pot of tea came out. 'This is OK,' I thought, 'how thoughtful of the owner to make a pot of tea just for me'. Within seconds doors started to open and five men appeared. They began rolling out the most dazzling coloured Indian carpets one could wish to see. They were being flung about in all directions. Then, of course, I got the message. They were trying to sell me a carpet. This was a deliberate act on Sunny's part to leave me in this shop. No doubt my friend Sunny would get his cut of the proceeds. The owner of the shop was very persistent. I then told him I sold life assurance and I already knew the answers to his questions. His face dropped. I could sense his dismay at not getting a sale. I certainly wasn't going to buy a carpet at this stage of my holiday. Maybe later, it depended on how the money lasted. I wasn't interested right now, I told him. The owner reluctantly allowed me to leave, but first he was to introduce me to the manager of the jeweller's shop next door. The same thing happened here - extreme pressure on me this time to buy a ring.. I made my excuses and left.

I walked out of the jeweller's and Sunny was very keen to take me to another shop, a clothes shop above the jeweller's. He took me to the counter that was selling ladies dresses, dozens of Indian saris and some Western clothes. The girl behind the counter was highly attractive with a big flashing smile.

"What's your name?" I asked.

"Sweety," she said.

"Your name's Sweety?" I replied.

"Yes, Sweety," she said. "What's wrong with Sweety, then?"

"Nothing, it's a nice name," I replied. I then said: "If I went up to a young girl in England and called her Sweety she might think I was getting fresh with her."

"Fresh - what's that?" she asked.

"Forget it," I said.

"I will forget only if you buy a scarf from me."

"Not this time Sweety," I replied. I then had to inform her that I had spent all my money during the day.

"But when I'm in Delhi again I'll definitely call on you," I said. Sweety smiled that same smile again. "Please do," she said. I really would have bought that scarf from her. I could sense her disappointment. These sales assistants really work hard to get a sale. I felt sorry for her. I felt I'd let her down.

One of the really enjoyable aspects of my first full day in India was that just about everyone I spoke to had a good command of the English language. It seems to be the second language here. Sunny was certainly near fluent in English and the shop owners and assistants were also quite fluent. Believe me, it helps.

How frustrating it has been taking holidays abroad and not being able to communicate with the people of that particular country because one can't speak the language. Here in India there's just not that problem. English is spoken widely here, and very good English, too.

It was now nearing five o'clock and Mr Singh picked us up with his Ambassador car. There really are hundreds of these British-style cars. I wonder why. On the journey back to my hotel I asked Sunny an intriguing question. This had bothered me all day. Everywhere we had been during my first day in India I had noticed young boys of about the 18-year age group holding hands while walking down any number of streets, just like a teenage boy and girl would do in England. To a Westerner like myself it was very noticeable.

"Why do young male couples hold hands?" I asked Sunny.

"Not illicit, my friend," he said, "Indian males have a great affection for each other. It is purely an innocent relationship, an expression of love between them, certainly not homosexual."

At the hotel I shook hands with Sunny and Mr Singh. It had been a rewarding day in many ways for someone like me, seeing India for the first time. I certainly had plenty to contemplate. Although I'd told the sales assistant in the clothes shop that all my money had gone, that wasn't exactly the truth - I had money for a tip for Sunny and Mr Singh. As I gave Sunny his tip, just for something to say and hoping, of course, that I'd given him enough, I said to him: "Shall I see you again?"

"Not in this world," he said. Then they were off, never to be seen again in this world, according to Sunny. It was a peculiar statement to make. Had I given him a big enough tip? This Indian money was strange to me. There was nothing I could do about it now. Tonight I would be in bed early, with an early call for 5am tomorrow. I'm off to Agra to see the Taj Mahal, one of the seven wonders of the world. I can't wait.

Day Three   10.11.91

Agra, Fatehpur Sikri, The Taj Mahal and Misery.

Early call this morning for 5.15am to catch the Shatabdi Express at 6.15am from Delhi railway station for a journey of nearly two hours to Agra. I was picked up at my hotel by a driver from the travel company at 5.30am. During the half-hour drive to the station I was surprised to see so many people about. At that time of the morning I expected the streets to be deserted apart from, say, the usual amount of people making their way to work - but not so here in Delhi. There were thousands of people about, some standing on pavements, some just waiting, it seemed, for something to happen. Waiting for what? I thought.

Admittedly the market stalls in the main streets were opening up, but where did these people come from and where were they going? This really intrigued me. Then in a flash it came to me. These thousands of people were hanging about because they had nowhere to go. This was their life. These people were the homeless of India, and there were millions of them. I had again seen another side of this country, I was learning something every minute. Those poor homeless people, how different their lives are to my own comfortable life. I can't get this poverty I keep seeing out of my mind and it hurts.

At the station it was even worse. I don't think I've ever seen so many people on a railway station. By their hundreds they were trying to sleep, curled up under a blanket of sorts. How they could sleep with all that noise going on I'll never know. The platform was full of bodies. Amid all the hustle and bustle I was stepping over people in order to get to the train which was waiting. So this is where the homeless sleep, I thought But these were the lucky ones. At least they had a roof over their heads - out on the streets they had no protection at all. The scene on this railway station reminded me of Richard Attenborough's marvellous film Gandhi. In the film there were several scenes in railway stations simply overcrowded with people. If Gandhi's ghost had appeared on this station this morning he would have fitted perfectly into the general scene.

As the Shatabdi Express pulled away from the station for Agra, the early morning light was beginning to break through. The train was air-conditioned and far superior to the average train seen in India. I had seen TV pictures of Indian trains packed to the rafters with arms and legs hanging outside the carriages. This train was not like that. This was the Shatabdi Express, one of the most luxurious trains on the Indian rail network. Advance bookings had to be made, tourists like myself were travelling to see the Taj Mahal. The journey was most pleasant, the countryside being very flat. On looking from the carriage window the colours of the Indian landscape struck me - a lovely mixture of green fields and trees and golden, sandy-looking ground. I was told by a fellow passenger that there was plenty of green about in the fields and trees because only a few weeks ago India was in the grip of the monsoon. The monsoon season, of course, brings rain, rain and even more rain. Without this excessive rain which comes but once a year, nothing would ever grow in the fields. The poor peasant farmer's life depends on the monsoon. Without it he would not survive.

The train journey from Delhi to Agra is about 130 miles and after a hearty breakfast it seemed the train was arriving in Agra station in no time at all. Here I was met by a guide who introduced himself as Amin. This station, just like Delhi, was packed with people. Outside I was to meet Mr Gupta the driver and to travel in yet another Morris Ambassador. Amin explained to me that as it had been raining in Agra since early that morning it would be better if first we went to Fatehpur Sikri, a deserted city only 22 miles west of Agra, and then see the Taj Mahal in all its glory later in the day, when hopefully it would be brighter. This was going to be one of the highlights of my stay in India, so far better to see it later when hopefully the sun would be out.

The Taj Mahal is one of the areas in India that tourists undoubtedly make for. Agra, although not an attractive city, has a history going back to 1501. Emperor Sikandar Lodi made it his capital and then another emperor, Akiba, made it the capital over Delhi. Then yet another emperor, the 17th century Jahangir, made it very much the centre of the Islamic world. Agra has monuments from its past going back many centuries. India's history has fascinated me. I didn't really realise it had such a compelling history. It wasn't until I knew I was coming here that I started reading about its history. I'm only getting fleeting glimpses of it, though. I only wish I had more time.

As we made our way to Fatehpur Sikri I was struck once again by the sheer mass of people, Agra being no exception, but what really took my eye - as in Delhi - was the sacred cow. Look down any high street and there she is, a majestic-looking beast who walks the streets of India as if she owns the place. Everything seems to stop for the cow. All the traffic in the cities simply goes round her. It could be the busiest street in the whole of India and it would be perfectly safe. The reason why the cow is so sacred is that it is the sacred cow of Hinduism. Cows out in the country areas pull ploughs and carts and paddle rice, often help to grind corn by pushing a small millstone round in a circle, and, of course, supply milk. Yes, the cow is very much part of India. The sacred cow is an institution and without it India would never be quite the same.

On the half-hour journey to Fatehpur Sikri from Agra by car I was quite disturbed by the treatment of big brown bears, who seemed to be on the route every five miles. What happens is that when an Indian spots a Morris Ambassador coming along he knows that it is a taxi with a tourist inside. To get the attention of the passenger he gets the bear up on its hind legs. A steel ring through its nose is attached to a rope which he holds and with a stick in his other hand he whips the poor old bear around the head and nose. The nose and jaw, incidentally, are muzzled. The bear has to stay on its hind legs while its owner walks it across the road, so that as the car passes it will often stop so that the tourist will, hopefully, give the owner some money. I know there are various ways a poor Indian has to survive in this country to make a living, but I found the treatment of these bears quite sickening. As our car passed these bears I could hardly look at them. They were old and probably had to go through this charade a hundred times a day. No way would I stop. This nauseating procedure happened every five miles and it made me weep.

Fatehpur Sikri is a magnificent deserted city, built in red stone. Emperor Akbar lived there and briefly made it his capital. On entering the Agra gate I was led by my guide Amin to the great courtyard, on to the pavilion, then to see the Turkish Sultana's house. Then I climbed the five-tiered Panch Mahal, a palace with superb views of the surrounding countryside. The great courtyard was often the scene of executions and torture. The story goes that Akbar had to abandon the city after 14 years because he was unable to get water to it. Standing as it does on high ground it would have been extremely difficult to get water there in the 15th century. So it stands today as if Akbar had only just left. He made it his commercial and administrative capital, but it is there for the tourist to see and it is certainly not to be missed.

Back in Agra we called to see the imposing Agra Fort, situated on the banks of the Yamuna River. Again, it was built by the Emperor Akbar. What history there is in these forts. We could not stay long, so we had a meal and made our way to the Taj Mahal. No words from me can describe what thousands of others have tried to describe. To me it was awe-inspiring. The sun was out by the time of our visit and there it stood in dazzling white. At dawn its colour changes from white to silver to rose pink and by sunset it is golden. The Taj Mahal was built from a man's love for a woman. At the death of his beloved wife Emperor Shah Jahan built a mausoleum of breathtaking beauty to enshrine her memory. It took more than 22 years to build. Built of white marble by a Persian architect it stands today in all its glory, in superb grounds and gardens. I had seen it and it really is one of the Seven Wonders of the World.

Just a small incident, but one that could have got out of control, happened on the steps outside the Taj Mahal. Amin had told me that no video cameras were allowed in the grounds and certainly not near or inside the Taj Mahal. Cameras were OK. All at once he became quite hysterical. Some tourist, and there were thousands there, was using his video camera only yards from the Taj. Amin went up to this person to tell him that this type of camera was not allowed. A heated argument developed. At one point the exchange of words became so aggressive that I could see myself being the innocent party in a punch-up. I would have to try to separate the two of them. A security guard came over to sort out this argument. Next thing, the video camera man was led away probably, as Amin told me, to be put outside the Taj Mahal grounds. I couldn't understand why Amin was so put out about this video camera. "Look," he says, "my living is made by showing people such as you round the Taj Mahal. Say that man had a bomb in his camera and the Taj was blown up. My living would be gone and I would be finished." I could see his point. This magnificent building must be protected at all costs. Amin was right. Without it there would be no tourist. I myself had taken lots of photographs. Only once in a lifetime does one get to see the Taj Mahal and I wanted a record of it.

After the visit to the Taj Mahal I was taken by Amin to a shop which sells tables, made, I was told, of the same marble as the Taj. We walked through the shop and into the workshop to be introduced to the manager, who then did his utmost to try to sell me a table. My guide Amin was obviously after some commission. It was the Sunny situation again, but I was having none of it and not for the first time I made a hurried exit from an Indian shop.

Amin, not finished yet, took me to a jeweller's shop in Agra. There were five assistants in this shop who appeared to be doing nothing. A white face in an Indian shop may give a mistaken impression of wealth. When I walked in, the assistants might have thought I'd come to buy the shop out. The manager saw me and rushed over. He may have thought I was an English millionaire businessman. He dived into the glass counter cabinet and out came with some of the most expensive-looking rings I'd ever seen. These rings were worth many thousands of pounds. All the assistants then gathered round me. As I stooped over the cabinet I tried one of the rings on my finger. I was now being crushed on all sides, excited shop assistants nearly jumping out of their skins. Was this, then, the mammoth sale they had been hoping for? I then tried on an even more expensive ring. I then said, "what's the cricket score?"

The manager was caught completely off guard. "Come into the office, sir, it's on TV," he said. I knew it was on TV because I had seen it on TV in various shops we had passed. Radios were also on full blast all over Agra. This really is a cricket-mad country. I sat down in an armchair in the manager's office. India were playing South Africa in a one-day international at Eden Gardens, Calcutta. I would be flying to Calcutta tomorrow. If I'd gone a day earlier, who knows, I might well have been at the match. I knew I couldn't sit in the manager's office too long. I didn't want to wear out my welcome, bearing in mind that I wasn't going to buy anything. The assistants were excited that India were winning. I made my exit quickly. Amin had put me in embarrassing position. I was not rich - far from it. I made the crack about the cricket score to ease the tension. Shop managers and assistants in India are very pushy, but I wasn't to be pushed and we were on our way.

It was six o'clock in the evening. Mr Gupta the driver took me to a hotel in Agra. He informed me he would pick me up in an hour. I needed a good clean-up. As I stepped from the filth and squalor of the streets, the very next second I was in the most luxurious hotel imaginable. I had stepped from one world into another. The hotel was full of tourists looking splendid in evening attire. One could close one's eyes and be in the Savoy in London. The contrast between a top hotel and filth outside is somewhat unbelievable here in India, but it does happen and continues to take me by surprise.

Feeling much cleaner after my wash and brush-up I ventured outside the hotel and stood at the gates. I just stood there taking in the general scene. Several rickshaw pullers came over to me. As I've said before, the average Indian can speak English and in no time the rickshaw pullers were talking to me - and in no time after that others joined in and there must have been about 20 Indians gathered round me. One little man, who seemed to be doing most of the talking offered me a cigarette. An Indian cigarette seems not much bigger than a matchstick. "I can't afford to smoke," I said. They all fell about laughing. Here was this man, they thought, who had just come out of this beautiful hotel and he can't afford to smoke. I had amused them greatly. "He can't afford to smoke," they laughingly repeated.

I then asked the little man who was by far the most talkative what his name was. "My name is Misery," he said with pride.

"Is that your real name?" I said.

"Yes, my name is Misery," he repeated.

Here am I in all the filth of Agra, where life is very hard and where some people just struggle to get through the day, and I ask someone his name and he says "Misery". I didn't know whether to laugh or cry. He looked at me, smiling across his face, not knowing the true meaning of the word. It was probably just as well.

Misery then started getting more excitable in his talk, although I couldn't pick up every word. He talked about something being done worldwide. What on earth is he talking about, I thought. He reeled off lots of countries, notably England, America, Germany, France and India. He was trying his hardest to make me understand.

"You know," he said, "woman", did I want a woman. If I did he would take me to one. No, no, I have a good woman at home, I said, to change the subject and not realising quite what I was about to say, I then said "How old's the boy?" A boy of about twelve had stood alongside Misery during all this time. I thought he was probably his son. Misery grinned·from ear to ear. He then looked at me in a most peculiar way. Then that smile flashed across his face again. Misery couldn't believe his luck.

"You want boy?" he said excitedly. I realised I'd asked completely the wrong question and I made my retreat back to the hotel.

Amin, who had been dropped off at his office by Mr Gupta after our visit to the jewellers shop, was in the car when I was picked up at the hotel. It was 7.30pm and the car made its way to Agra railway station. There were crowds of people there, of course, then when the train arrived everyone seemed to make a dash for it. My seat was reserved, so there was no rush for me. I shook hands with Amin, who had been an excellent guide. Just like Sunny in New Delhi he knew his subject, and I was better for it. I then gave both him and Mr Gupta a tip. I also shook hands with Mr Gupta, who was such a gentle man. He told me in conversation during the day that he was working all hours so he could send his son to university. "I want him to make a better life than me," he had said.

On the train taking me back to New Delhi, which had left at 8pm, I quickly got talking to a Mr Shaw, an Indian insurance and financial counsellor for the Indian government. He had his wife and two children with him and came from Bombay. As we were both insurance people we hit it off straight away. We wanted to know about each other's work. Could I get him an agency with my company in India, he asked. I said I would inquire for him. He gave me his card, which I find happens regularly here. Talk to any businessman and he will give you his card. When one receives a card of this nature one is touched by the sincerity of it all. Indian people really are a friendly people. They are extremely courteous and helpful at all times. Giving a business card is their way of breaking down any barriers that may exist between you and them.

Having said how friendly the Indians are, a porter on the train tried to charge me four Rupees for a bottle of pop. Mr Shaw pointed out to me that I would have to pay for this drink - for four Rupees I was not going to argue. I naturally thought that all food and drink given to me was already paid for. Mr Shaw said, "I don't think so." The porter then came and asked for four Rupees and Mr Shaw gave him a ticking off, calling him a cheat and a liar. The argument got very heated. For the second time in a day I could sense trouble brewing, with me in the middle of it. If only to keep the peace, another railway official then appeared and things quietened down. He then gave the porter a dressing down and the porter hurried off like a naughtly schoolboy. He had been shamed over just four Rupees. I couldn't believe it. Mr Shaw said, "Some Indians give this country a bad name."

On approaching Delhi station all at once I thought what on earth would I do if there was not a representative from my travel company there to meet me and take me to my hotel. To be alone on Delhi station at ten o'clock at night was asking for trouble. I expressed my fears to Mr Shaw. He would look after me, he said. On arrival it looked more crowded than ever. Eventually a friendly face appeared - the driver who picked me up when I first arrived at New Delhi airport. Mr Shaw would only leave me when I convinced him that this was indeed the man who I recognised. I was thankful for him. He was a real gentleman, Indian through and through, but with an English name. He was the type that gives India a good name. We shook hands and he was gone and lost in the crowd.

I got back to my hotel in New Delhi at 10.45pm. It had been quite a day. I had a lot to reflect on. Thinking of my friend Mr Shaw on the train, we were reflecting on our families. Had I a daughter? he asked.

"Yes," I said.

"Is she married?" he wanted to know.

"Yes, I am a grandfather," I said, feeling quite proud.

"Did you arrange her marriage?" he asked.

I smiled to myself. My daughter Julie would certainly not have wished for father to have arranged her marriage. In India marriages are arranged by parents as their children are growing up. Did these marriages work? Hopefully I would learn more about this subject during my stay.

I've just finished writing about my day's events and it's past midnight. Tomorrow I fly to Calcutta, a place that had always intrigued me. Was it really as bad as English soldier and colonial administrator Robert Clive's description of it as the most wicked place in the universe? He made that statement well over 200 years ago, and by all accounts it hasn't changed that much since. I didn't have to go to Calcutta when my itinerary was being drawn up. It was in the north east of the country. I could so easily have flown from New Delhi to Ranchi, but Calcutta I had to see. Centuries ago it was known as the Black Town. I couldn't wait to see it. Don't ask me why - curiosity, I suppose. But before that I have another dreaded flight. Let's get it over with, I thought. Tomorrow is another day.

Day Four 11.11.91

Trouble at Dum Dum Airport

Up at 7am. At the breakfast table I talked to one of the waiters. He was anxious to talk to me. He wanted to get married. Pay was so poor at this hotel and in India generally, he informed me. He then tells me he wants to come to England. What are the prospects of finding a job, he asks. He also tells me he has qualifications.

"I want to get married, but the pay is so poor here - how can I?" he asks. I had to tell him there was a lot of unemployment in England at present and that it would be unwise for him to come over just now.

"No future here," he says again. He walked away in total disillusionment. I wish I could have been more helpful, but I was only being honest.

A different driver from the travel company picked me up at the hotel - we were off to the airport. It's a wonder we ever got there - so much traffic, which the majestic sacred cow once again seemed to control. How infuriating for the drivers of all these vehicles she must be. If the cow is sacred, then the other animals roaming the streets certainly are not. I am thinking in particular of stray dogs. Every pavement has a dog. I've never seen such unhappy-looking animals. Some are so thin that their ribs really stand out. As they scratch about for food nobody looks at them. They are like lepers, ignored and despised. Certainly, nobody would ever stroke a dog - to see the sores on its body makes that understandable. At home I have a dog called Slippy. It has been pampered by all the family. It would simply not survive on these streets. It would take one look at this place, have a heart attack and die.

At New Delhi International Airport there is very tight security. The terrorist situation is very much in evidence here - double-checks on all packages, suitcases etc., security guards everywhere. The tension is already building up for me. This very tight security gives me the creeps. In no time I am a passenger on the bus to the aircraft. What a huge monster it looks as I step off the bus and walk up the stairway into the 'plane. On this Indian Airways flight no. IC401 I strap myself tightly into my seat. Does it really matter whether one is tightly strapped in or not, I ask myself. The dreaded engines start up and down the runway we go. I am actually writing these notes right now. Speed is increasing by the second, my hands are sweating, so much so that I can hardly hold my pen. The aircraft now lifts up and away we go, climbing and climbing into the clouds. I'm in God's hands again. I'm sweating like a pig. My fears recede as the Indian air hostess brings on the food. What a beautiful girl she is. The last thing I want, though, is food. Writing 30 minutes later, I have changed my mind and have eaten. I must be getting used to Indian food, very hot and spicey. I miss my Yorkshire pudding, though. While waiting for this flight in New Delhi I bought the Hindustan Times newspaper. It tells of an emergency landing by an aircraft only yesterday at Calcutta Airport. I can only sit here and pray.

The front page news in all the English-speaking newspapers is all about India's victory in the one-day cricket international yesterday against South Africa. This three-match series has created an enormous amount of interest. India were due to play Pakistan. The tour of India had actually started, but it was only a few days old when Pakistan felt obliged to call it off because of violence by Hindu militants. A game between the two countries was due to be played at Bombay's Wankhede Stadium, but the pitch was dug up and oil poured over it. Tension between Hindu India and Islamic Pakistan runs deep. Wars have been fought between the two countries, the most recent in 1971. A mere cricket match between them is not just a game. "Muslim blood cannot be sacrificed for a game of cricket," said the sports minister of Pakistan, so the tour was called off.

With the tour being called off, India then invited South Africa to fill the gap left by Pakistan. South Africa have recently been re-admitted into world cricket after a gap of 21 years. The evil Apartheid rules are being lifted in South Africa and because of this the world cricket authorities decided by an overwhelming majority that South Africa be allowed to play international cricket again. I for one was pleased. Apartheid should never, in my opinion have been a reason for not playing South Africa at sport. Sport should have no barriers. The world was only too pleased to trade with South Africa - why a sports ban, I ask. Talk about double standards. Apartheid is evil. I'm sure most fair-minded people would agree. Hypocrisy was certainly preached about the whole South Africa issue. In some countries of the world people are being persecuted. These countries have a dismal record on human rights, yet they have always been quick to attack South Africa. My answer is that people in glass houses should not throw stones.

The aircraft has been in the air one-and-a-half hours. Right now I am in the skies above the state of Bihar, where Albina lives. It's because of her that I'm making this journey. She must be getting excited now. In her last letter to me in July, when she knew I was to visit her, she said she was counting the days. We live in a strange world. I'm travelling thousands of miles to see someone I have never met. Through letters between us a friendship has been struck up. I've no real fears we shan't get on. I feel as though I've already met her. I have these thoughts as the aircraft begins to descend into Calcutta Airport.

The flight took over one hour, 55 minutes, a perfect flight and a perfect landing into Dum Dum Airport. What utter relief. I feel born again, all tensions gone. As I came off the 'plane I immediately noticed the difference in temperature - considerably warmer and more humid, I thought. It felt good to be in the fresh air again, but I wasn't quite ready for what was about to happen next. What I did was done out of innocence. Through my own stupidity I was nearly arrested.

As I came down the aircraft steps I had got about 50 yards from the 'plane when I turned round and took a photograph of it. All hell broke loose. People started shouting at me. What's wrong, what's going on, I thought. Why are these fellow passengers shouting at me? I've only taken a photograph.

"You cannot take photographs here," someone shouted. Within seconds a security guard appeared. He was very aggressive.

"No photos," he kept saying. "Give me that camera," he shouted. I argued with him. I tried to tell him I was doing no harm. "No photos," he said again. "This is a top-security airport," I understood him to say. He was very excitable, with a gun on a sling. He seemed very jumpy - nervous is probably the correct word. All his ramblings were in very poor English. I couldn't pick up everything he said, and I thought I was about to be arrested. I couldn't argue with a gun, so rather than hand over the camera I gave him the film. He snatched it from me. As he walked away he was tearing up the film in his rage. A friend at home had warned me not to take photographs at Indian airports. I had disregarded his warning and I was annoyed with myself.

As I walked to the airport building I then realised that the 20 or so photographs taken at the Taj Mahal yesterday were on that film which the security guard had taken from me. This made me even more annoyed with myself. I would, in all probability, never have the opportunity to see the Taj Mahal again. I would never have my own photographs of it. I could have kicked myself. I had seen one of the Seven Wonders of the World and I had no evidence to say I had. How utterly stupid I'd been. I only had myself to blame.

After walking through the airport building and on collecting my luggage I was met outside by a rep from the travel company with a sign saying "Mr Holdich". There were lots of people outside the airport with these boards with names on. I went up to this man, who introduced himself as Chandra. I climbed into yet another Morris Ambassador car and was driven to my hotel. On this short ride I saw lots of mud hovels called bustees, lots of tin or wood-roofed buildings which are people's homes. Thousands live this way, I was told. They are no more than shacks, really. I could see people squatting inside these bustees. Could people really live in these places, I thought. What I saw throught that car window was human degradation on an incomparable scale. I thought I'd seen enough squalor and filth in New Delhi and Agra. What I was seeing here was worse. This was deprivation on a much larger scale, which I hadn't seen before. How could people survive here, I thought. The beggars were on the streets, children with fear in their eyes and looking so under-nourished. I was seeing poverty on an unbelievable scale. This, then, was Calcutta. I was here and there was no turning back.

The car pulled up at the Kenelworth Hotel. Chandra took me into the foyer to check in. It was lovely and cool inside - the hotel was air-conditioned. This again reminded me of the other hotels I'd seen in India. I had once again stepped into another world. One second filth and shanty towns, the next I was with the privileged of this world, myself included. People were starving and dropping dead right outside the hotel gates. Inside this hotel Western holidaymakers and businessmen were drinking and laughing and indulging in lifetime habits of good food and smug living, seemingly oblivious to what was going on outside. I can't help thinking this world of ours is so unfair at times. The destitute of this city can't help being born into appalling poverty. I've always considered myself one of the lucky ones of this world. If I didn't know this before I came to India I certainly do now.

After a hot shower and something to eat I decided to stay in the hotel for the evening. It's now six o'clock and the city is in darkness. Darkness comes early on the sub-continent. As I write my notes for the day I think of this city and what I shall see tomorrow. I know I shall see even more poverty. Perhaps some of it will be too unbearable to look at, but I've got to see it. What is Calcutta really like. Tomorrow I intend to find out.

Day Five   12.11.91

Oh Calcutta And Eden Gardens

"I shall always be glad to have seen it, for the reason that it will be unnecessary for me ever to see it again."

Winston Churchill, writing to his mother about Calcutta.

After a good night's sleep - I was in bed by 10.15pm - I did not know the time this morning, so I had to phone reception. My watch had stopped. Breakfast was very basic - four rounds of toast and three cups of tea. Four Indian waiters were just standing around, waiting on my every whim. I'm told their pay is extremely low. But one of the reasons for low wages is overstaffing. The staff in this hotel could easily be cut by half. If hotels like this employed fewer staff they could pay higher wages, but if they did that, jobs would be lost. At least this way it gives people who would never normally stand a chance of employment some work and dignity.

At 9am I was picked up at my hotel in Russel Street by my guide Chandra and a day's tour of Calcutta was arranged. The driver of the car couldn't speak a word of English and Chandra wasn't very good at the language either. At times I failed to understand what he was really talking about. He was, in my opinion, not an experienced guide like the ones I had had in New Delhi and Agra. Calcutta is a city of more than 12 million people. Obviously, I wanted to be told as much about the place as possible. To say Chandra was a disappointment is perhaps a true description of him. I had the impression he wanted the tour over as quickly as possible. I felt slightly let down by him.

This city numbs the senses. What I saw on this day's tour hits a westerner between the eyes. Oh, Calcutta, I thought. The garbage and sheer squalor is at times unbelievable. But having said that, maybe - just maybe - I'm getting used to seeing constant filth. I wasn't quite so affected as I might have been. Yes, it was bad, intolerable in fact. The poverty was on a much larger scale than in New Delhi. There seemed to be a lot more beggars on the streets. The look in one poor woman's eyes I shall remember for months to come. She had a baby in her arms and she was so very grateful to me when I gave her some Rupees. What I couldn't get over was how surprisingly beautiful she was.

She had followed Chandra and me as we walked through the streets. "No money, no money. Please, please." There was a desperation in her voice. She tugged at my shirt in this desperation. Until this moment I hadn't looked at her properly. Chandra beckoned our driver, who was following behind us. Just before I stepped into the car I gave her five Rupees. Once in the car I turned to look at her. She was dressed in rags, with her poor baby dressed likewise, yet underneath those ragged clothes was a strikingly beautiful woman. She had classic looks, and here she was begging on the streets. If that woman had walked through the streets of my home city of Peterborough she would have turned many heads. Looking clean and wearing different clothes she would have stopped the traffic. She was absolutely stunning. She was about 21 years of age. It has crossed my mind that she might not make it to the age of 22.

I had noticed so often since arriving in India that the really desperately poor women looked quite vivacious, particularly the Bengali women of Calcutta. I'm sure that when I looked really closely I could see Ava Gardner in all of them. Yet the prosperous Indians who had, in all probability, made their money from the poor in this city, had lost their looks - or whatever good looks they may have had. So much for high living, I thought. The wealthy have abused their bodies with fat food and excessive drinking, and it showed. How annoying it must be for the rich to have the wealth, but not the looks to go with it. How infuriating for them.

Chandra took me to the Queen Victoria Hall. Outside this magnificent white-stoned building is the Queen Victoria statue. The building is now a museum. On walking round it one automatically thinks of the British Raj. What an influence the British must have had on this country. Mistakes were obviously made, thousands killed in the making of India. But the pictures on the walls of that museum gave evidence of what India had won and lost in the field of battle. The British Raj is still in India. Walk in that museum and the atmosphere is there. One can smell it and see it. And if one cocks one's ear, one can nearly hear it.

We then walked in the Maidan, which is a spacious green belt about three miles long. All over this vast stretch of green kids were playing cricket, hundreds of different games going on, no doubt trying to emulate their hero, the swashbuckling Kapil Dev. He is idolised in India - with his Omar Sharif looks he can do no wrong.

At the end of the Maidan is the Calcutta Racing Club, probably the oldest club in Calcutta. Its meetings have been attended by royalty and other visiting dignitaries. Polo has been played in the central oval since 1861. As I peeped through the steel fence to gaze up at the big stands I sensed that horse racing was very much for the rich - an exclusive club, if you like. Perhaps I'm wrong, but what I do know is that the lower castes in this city would not be let anywhere near the place. The only time they would be allowed in would be when they were cleaning the place up for the next meeting.

In the car we make our way to the Hooghly River. A new bridge is being built...not so new, though. It has had construction and strike troubles ever since it was started over ten years ago. Both sides of the bridge have been built, but with a big hole of about two hundred yards in the middle. Maybe waiting for the two ends to join will take another ten years. Also to be seen further up river is the mighty Haora Bridge, built by the British over 60 years ago. The river, incidentally, looked foul with pollution, really dirty and muddy. Indians bathe in this river every day. They might possibly come out of the River Hooghly far dirtier than when they went in. If Indians are not cleaning themselves in the river one can see them in the streets gathered round a standpipe. Indians really are a clean people. They should be, because they spend hours just doing that.

On leaving the river we drove by a massive stadium. There it was, the Eden Gardens cricket ground, before my very eyes. Being a keen follower of the game, my wife would say cricket mad, I just knew I had to see the ground.

"Stop the car," I said to Chandra. The driver stopped and out I jumped. I walked up to the massive frontage of this huge stadium and knocked on what appeared to be the secretary's office window.

"Can I have a look inside," I enquired as a window was opened.

"Afraid not. Nobody allowed in, very tight security," the man at the window said.

I noticed when he said those words that he kept looking at my camera. They seem to think that all cameras carry bombs. I tried to convince him that I had no intention of blowing up Eden Gardens.

"Look," I said, "I've come thousands of miles from England to see this ground. I won't go away until I see it." He could see I was pleading with him. His attitude changed.

"Alright, but only for a few minutes," he said.

The main gates were opened and Chandra and I walked through them into the pavillion and out onto the ground. As I walked out onto the hallowed turf the feelings I got were like an electric current surging through my body. Talk about hairs standing up on the back of my neck. This was indeed one of the greatest cricket grounds in the world. As I walked to the square, for non-cricketing people the centre of the ground, I'm sure my legs began to wobble. This ground was an imposing structure with massive stands as far as the eye could see, but not like a football stadium, which is often a mass of concrete and little else. This stadium had its own cricket atmosphere. It was made for cricket. Only two days ago 95,000 were in this ground watching a one-day international between India and South Africa. What on earth can the atmosphere have been like? I thought of all the great players in world cricket who had played here. What must it be like to score a century here? I would die a happy man if I could play just one game here. This ground is the Taj Mahal of cricket. It is quite simply awe-inspiring. While out in the middle Chandra took several photographs for me. At this point the security guard who had been watching beckoned us to come off the ground. My few minutes were up. I could quite willingly have stayed there all day. Whenever I go to Lord's cricket ground in London I have these feelings that I've had today. The game of cricket is in my blood, I've been hooked on it all my life. I had seen the magnificent Eden Gardens cricket ground and I will be eternally grateful. What a difference between Outgang Road and Eden Gardens. Where's Outgang Road, you may well ask. It is the home of Market Deeping Cricket Club. When I next play cricket at Outgang Road I shall close my eyes and think of Eden Gardens. I shall be in heaven, because Eden Gardens is my idea of heaven.

Back to the car and Chandra did his best to describe Calcutta. There are good guides and bad guides. He pointed out several landmarks, but I could see he wasn't too interested. While walking this afternoon two children pulled at my shirt. This happens frequently in Indian cities.

"No mama, no papa," they cried. They wouldn't leave me. I gave them some Rupees. They were the street kids of Calcutta and there are thousands of them. Chandra made a dash for the car to get away from those children and I followed. They were two of the loveliest looking children one could wish to see, their lives mapped out for them - a life of begging on the streets. They would be about six years old, surviving on the streets with thousands of others. If they didn't beg or steal they wouldn't survive; And if there's no survival it's death.

Chandra dropped me off at the hotel. It was four o'clock and I would see him again when he picked me up on Friday to take me to the airport for my flight to Ranchi. I had a shower and wasn't I dirty. Calcutta in parts is filthy, believe me. I now had two whole days left in Calcutta and I was pondering what to do with them. I had two alternatives. Was I going to venture out on my own and accept the consequences of walking on my own in this city of teeming millions? Afterall I was white, on my own and an easy target. Or would I stay in my hotel, frightened to go out alone, and wait for the Friday to catch my next 'plane.

I decided to take the bull by the horns, as it were. I would go out alone and walk the streets. I couldn't be a prisoner in my hotel. I wanted to see more of this city. Admittedly, the poverty appalled me, but I was being gripped in a peculiar way. Amid all this human degradation I really did find that Calcutta had a soul - and an even bigger heart. I had noticed that deep within this city, just below the surface, that people who lived here laughed in the face of adversity. If one lived in this place one had to have a sense of humour. It was one of the ways of surviving and they managed it. Well, some of them did.

Day Six   13.11.91

The Black Hole

Hardly slept at all last night. Bangs going off all night, just like fireworks. One loud bang seemed to shake the hotel. It was just as though a terrorist's bomb had gone off. When I try to get to sleep at home I can hear every noise, so what chance have I here? - and I take sleeping tablets. What the bangs were and where they came from I don't know, but they certainly kept me awake.

Calcutta is the capital of West Bengal. It is the largest of all Indian cities in population and growing by the thousands. I suppose it must be extremely difficult to give a true figure of the number of people actually living here, but by all accounts it is now over 12 million. It is synonymous with poverty and squalor. It used to be the second largest city in the old British Empire after London. Calcutta was once the capital of India until government headquarters was moved to New Delhi in 1911. It was founded on a swamp by Job Charnock, an Englishman who built a warehouse for the East India Company, but real growth did not start until 1774. I wonder what Job Charnock's thoughts would be if he could see it now.

When I decided to come to Calcutta I was most interested in the history of the Black Hole. This tragic piece of history in Britain's great past always fascinated me. One learnt of it at school. The Black Hole of Calcutta became a casual name for any stuffy, overcrowded place. It got its notoriety in 1756, when a large Indian army attacked the fortress of Fort William

- an unthinkable act. The British, in their stupidity, were not really allerted to the attack and when they did wake up it was too late - Fort William was taken. Thousands had died. The Nawab of Bengal, Siraj-Ud-Daula-Siraj, who hated the British, had a fanatical desire to fight them - and fight them he did. The fort, poorly defended, fell in four days.

It was one of the most dramatic events in British Imperial history. It was a tragedy of errors which need never have happened. The British never thought in their worst nightmares that Fort William could be taken, just as, 180 years later, they never thought Singapore would fall to the Japanese. The British expected them to attack from the sea and pointed all their big artillery that way. Instead the Japanese came down from the north and caught the British off guard. Fort William and the fall of Singapore were terrible, tragic events in British history.

The Black Hole story goes that while the fighting was going on 145 Englishmen and one woman were forced into a dungeon measuring 18 feet by 14 by the Nawab's officers. The dungeon was no bigger than the average living room. It was a grim stone building. This happened on just about the hottest night of the year - well over 100 degrees. What agonies they must have gone through from the sheer heat. And they were packed so tightly that they were actually sitting on top of each other as the big wooden door was forced shut by the Nawab's officers. In the morning, when the fighting was over and the door was opened, 22 people had managed to survive. The dead had died from suffocation. The whole incident so outraged Britain that revenge was demanded. Robert Clive became a great hero when his army was sent to punish the Nawab. The forces of Siraj-Un-Daula and Clive's met on the battlefield on June 23, 1757.

Clive won a great victory and became Governor of Bengal.

This morning, therefore, I decided to find the original site of Fort William. In its place now is the big general post office on the west side of Dalhousie Square. There is supposed to be a plaque marking the spot of the Black Hole, but I was unable to find it. There is little else to remind one of this tragic incident. Only in the centre of Dalhousie Square opposite the post office will you find something from the past, in the shape of what was called the Great Tank. The Great Tank is a square ornamental pond surrounded by flower gardens, this being the area where English families used to take their evening walks from their Victorian-style houses which fronted what today is known as The Park. The Park is there now with its memories of what happened on that fateful day.

Although the garrison of Fort William was ill-prepared for such an attack by ravaging Indians, it is surprising how the fort managed to hold out for four days - afterall the garrison could only call on about 500 men against 50,000 Indians. The British certainly had cowards in their ranks, who fled down the Houghly River when the going got tough. They also had young men who defended the fort to their last breath and died heroes.

When the fighting stopped next morning and the door of the dungeon was opened the bodies of those who had died were put on a cart and dumped in The Park, but I'd read there was a monument to the dead in the churchyard of St John's Church. I eventually found this church, after walking many miles, and there in the churchyard was the monument nearly covered over by tree branches and looking derelict. All the names were there. I stood in silence for several minutes. For as long as I could remember I had been intrigued by the whole ghastly affair. Little did I think all those school days ago that I would come to Calcutta to delve into one of the worst incidents in the whole great British Empire's history.

On walking along the Chowringhee Nehru Road I was eating a bunch of bananas (and how I love those bananas) when I felt a hand touch mine. It was the same young boy and his sister, with two other children of about the same age, who I'd met yesterday. If one befriends Calcutta kids one has friends for life. They looked so pathetic that I just had to buy them something to eat.

"No mama, no papa," they cried. They then proceeded to follow me everywhere that afternoon. Soon several other children just tagged along. Several Indians came over to me to ask if the children were bothering me. To pacify the children I promised I would walk this way again tomorrow. One Indian man really bellowed at them to leave me alone. Eventually they allowed me to leave them. I had felt sorry for them. What Westerner wouldn't be?

On walking away from the children I thought of what sort of life was in store for them. I was beginning to get quite attached to those first two who spotted me. Have you ever seen kids who are desperate for food and clothing with no one to care for them. Well, I have. I worried what future there was for them. There are more than 500,000 beggars on the streets of Calcutta. Many are children. These children sleep on the pavements, they have no schooling, they beg, they steal. "No mama, no papa," they say. I shudder to think of their lives as they grow up. I read recently that there are more prostitutes in Calcutta than in any other city in the world. I feel for all the beggars here, but for children with their lives in front of them it's worse. Prostitution beckons. At home I have a four-month-old grandson. I can't help thinking how different his life will be -

loving parents, doting grandparents, all the Western world advantages of good health, schooling, etc. Here in Calcutta these kids have nothing. Prostitution, drugs, crime - you name it, they have every chance of doing it.

This tangled mass of people is never-ending. Just imagine coming out of a football match in England where one is shoulder to shoulder with people, often being pushed along. That's the best way I can describe the situation here. The Bengali Indian has a great sense of humour and they really are a friendly people. I'm forever chatting with them in this crowded city. I have seen very few white faces, but I feel perfectly at home here. Accept Calcutta for what it is and it will accept you. Accept the poverty - this is how I've managed my stay here. If one lets it get through to one, all this degradation and filth will make one's stay miserable. Admittedly I have been given some strange looks - one white face among thousands - but this city of rust and corrosion has accepted me and I am thankful.

I've walked miles today, this being by far the best way to see the city. During my walks I saw hundreds of posters of Lenin plastered all over it. With the world gradually rejecting Communism, this place seems to thrive on it. This is a Communist-controlled city. If Communism offers equal opportunities then, who knows, if it works the right way it could be the saviour of Calcutta. I saw long queues of people going to meetings in several areas, usually with Lenin's face on a poster outside the buildings, as if he was beckoning the people to come inside. But Communism has often failed in the past. Probably out of desperation, the people of Communist countries have demanded a change, Russia and Romania to name but two. Of course, corrupt leaders haven't helped. Communism might work in Calcutta, but everywhere else the system is breaking down.

On walking back to my hotel I looked inside a temple. I was not impressed by what I saw. I shuddered when I thought that animals are sacrificed in the name of religion. Far be it for me to comment on Indian religions, and there are literally hundreds of different religions here. I must have walked a good ten miles today - Harrison Street, Cotten Street, Central Avenue, so many British names all over this impoverished city. The city buildings are in a very poor condition, nearly falling down, some of them. Everywhere seemed derelict. The Morris Ambassador car is everywhere in Calcutta. I've read that these cars are now being made in Calcutta and sold to countries like England. Strange, isn't it. Over the years we have sold the Indians this car, now it's being sold back to us. Amongst all this traffic are the cart pullers and rickshaw pullers, going about their daily business, the cart pullers hoping to be carting goods, and the rickshaw pullers, who have a dreadfully hard life giving lifts to people all over Calcutta and charging about one Rupee for a couple of miles.

Calcutta is very much a cosmopolitan city. Radical Bengalis or intellectuals are ready to talk about any subject on this earth. Many of the better-off Bengalis have travelled over many areas of India. The millions who live here are often those who have made their home here. Calcutta's population continues to grow at an alarming rate. A figure of 15 million is quite possible in five to ten years time. Why does it grow at this pace? Workers from the state of Bihar, which is nextdoor to West Bengal, come here to seek work. Thousands of them have settled here. Of all the millions of people in Calcutta today only a very small percentage manage to find work. Also, Calcutta hasn't been helped in any way by the thousands of refugees who have come over from neighbouring Bangladesh. This country is even poorer than India. Why is it, I often ask myself, that these poverty-stricken Third World countries have had some of the most appalling tragedies, like earthquakes and flooding on a gigantic scale? Some questions can never be answered. Thousands of people have died recently in Bangladesh in great floods which have covered many areas of the country. We in the West only read of these tragedies in our newspapers. Out here in the sub-continent it is very real indeed.

I arrived back at my hotel for 5pm. Again I am absolutely filthy. Having had a long walk today I've decided I'll have an even longer walk tomorrow. I enjoy walking and seeing this city. Walking through its slums is, to me, the best possible way of seeing Calcutta. To sum up today, then: It has been a day full of interest. This city is infectious, it grows on one. Again I've seen more human misery than I'm ever likely to see, and destitution and malnutrition on a colossal scale, and all I can say is that it grows on one. I can't get enough of it. Calcutta is to me something special and I can't put my finger on why this should be. I love walking through this broken down city, I love mingling with its thousands on the streets. There is humour out there which has taken me completely by surprise. On reading so much about Calcutta before I came here I really did fear the worst. So roll on tomorrow, I want to see more of it.

Day Seven 14.11.91

Mother Teresa And The Street Kids

Today I have had the honour of meeting someone who, in my opinion, is one of the greatest human beings of the 20th century. She is the very frail 80-year-old lady known as the Angel of Calcutta, who cares for the dying destitute of this city. I have to pinch myself to make sure it wasn't a dream and that it really happened. But it did. To have seen this very special lady would have been a memory by itself, but to have talked to her for fully five minutes, just the two of us, is something else. But I am rushing ahead with today's events. I'll start at 9.30am, which is when I left my hotel.

I called at the really beautiful St Paul's Cathedral. Built in 1847, it's a serene stone building. It was evidently built along the same lines as St Martin in the Fields in London. A friend of mine has a great passion for churches. Wherever he goes he will visit one. Churches in England are our heritage, he says. I've now developed this into a passion myself. I love the peace and tranquility of a church. Also, no two churches are alike. Standing inside this St Paul's Cathedral was as though I was in a church in England. I also went inside St Andrew's Church. These churches were British-built, like so many other buildings in Calcutta. One cannot get away from the old country.

Next I walked along the Kidepore Road and finished up at the mighty Haora Bridge. This bridge over the Hooghly River is a massive steel structure, a real landmark of Calcutta. There were thousands of people on it and it was shaking - yes, a slight shake in the bridge because of the mass of people on it. I very much doubt if there is a bridge anywhere in the world which takes so many people on it during a day. This bridge has stood the test of time. Built by the British, it looks good for a few more years yet. Near the bridge and underneath the flyover I saw mud hovels, or were they shacks, known as Bustees. These Bustees are all over Calcutta in their thousands. To Western eyes living conditions look intolerable. To describe them as being like a cowshed is perhaps being kind. An English cowshed is clean by comparison. How people live in those conditions I'll never know. Most bustees I saw were absolutely filthy. I again felt sorry for the poor children, so skinny and undernourished. And the disease there must be in these bustees - cholera, dysentry and tuberculosis to name but a few...Babies eveidently die in shocking numbers. I'm not surprised. But somehow people survive. People in England should see what I've seen. It's really unbelievable at times. The very poorest families in England live like lords in comparison to people here. There are no poor in England on this scale.

On walking near the Writers Building I'm drawn into conversation with a schoolteacher from Goa, which is in south India. He tells me he has packed in his teaching job in Goa to try his luck in Calcutta, but is most disillusioned because he can't get a job anywhere.

"This Communist government here in Calcutta are all bent," he informs me. "The party leader has shares in all the big companies. Some Communist he is," he says. Then, out of the blue, he says: "You're English."

"Yes, I am," I say.

"Then would you like to meet Mother Teresa?" he asks.

"Yes, that would be very nice," I say. So, off we go to meet Mother Teresa. It was too good an opportunity to miss. I'm not sure whether I believed this man, but I would at least give it a try. I had time on my hands and, evidently, so did he.

Just before we arrived at Mother Teresa's, which took about half an hour, an incident happened which I know now I should never have been drawn into. On approaching South Street cemetery the man asked me if I wanted to go inside - I was bound to find it interesting, he said, because all British people were buried there. It was 50 years since the last burial here. In the cemetery one once again thinks of the British Raj. It had been kept reasonably tidy. I suppose if the ghost of the British Raj remains, then in this cemetery was where any ghosts might be. All at once, however, I felt very vulnerable with this man. It quickly went through my mind that I could have been well and truly set up. One minute we were deep in conversation, the next he seemed to be lagging behind me. I became suspicious. All conversation had dried up between us. Here I was, right in the middle of this city of millions in a deserted cemetery. I had a sixth sense that something was going to happen. He could have plunged a knife into me and I'd have been one of the thousands who go missing in this city.

"Come on," I said, "take me to Mother Teresa's." I walked away from him in quick time. If he was going to attack me and throw a knife between my shoulder blades this would be the time to do it. After what seemed like an eternity I got to the cemetery gates and safety. I was sweating - you bet I was. I thought how stupid I'd been to be talked into going into a cemetery by a total stranger. It was foolish in the extreme.

Once outside the cemetery I took a long look at this man. He was a real shifty-looking character. I could certainly not trust him again. As we made our way to Mother Teresa's, which was about ten minutes' walk from the cemetery, he informed me that he wished to go back to Goa. When we arrived at Mother Teresa's he obviously wanted a tip, so I gave him ten Rupees.

"This won't get me back to Goa," he said ungratefully. I told him ten Rupees was fair payment for bringing me here. After all if a person were to dig into his pocket every time he passed a beggar in the street, and for every so-called favour done by people like this man, a person like myself could soon be broke. I thanked him again and he went off very disgruntled. If looks could kill, I'd have been a dead man.

The approach to Mother Teresa's is down one of the many thousands of little back alleys found everywhere in Calcutta. When I got to the orangey red entrance door with Mother Teresa's name on it I was reluctant to knock. A young boy who was hanging around outside urged me to knock.

"Go on, knock. She will see you," he said. I then wondered what on earth I was doing there. I was certainly interested in Mother Teresa, but I'd not been sent by anyone to see her and I carried no message, so why, I thought, would she want to see me? I took a long, deep breath and knocked on the door and thought what a cheek I'd got.

The door opened and a young nun said "can I help you."

"I've come to see Mother Teresa," I stammered out.

" Do come inside," she said. I stepped inside and was led up some steps by another young sister. On reaching the top we turned into a large room. I then realised it was a chapel with a cross in the centre and religious pictures on the walls. We walked out of the chapel and just outside the door the sister told me to wait. I looked to my right and I could see Mother Teresa in conversation with another sister. On catching my eye she gently lifted her arm and acknowledged me.

After a few minutes she came over to me. She was all hunched up, a very frail old lady indeed. She greeted me like a long-lost nephew who she hadn't seen for a number of years. It's difficult to explain how I felt as with both hands she took mine. She made me sit down with her and she continued to hold my hands. I felt I was in a great presence. Mother Teresa's work with the poor in this city is well-known. She cares for the dying destitutes. Rather than die in the streets some make it to her orphanage or are taken there, she being a Catholic who cares for all, irrespective of religion, colour or creed. She founded her Missionaries of Charity in the Lower Circular Road in Calcutta in 1948. Her order has 300 houses in 70 countries, with as many as 150-odd in India. I was in the company of a world-famous human being. I had to pinch myself to believe it was really happening.

She was born in Albania in 1910 and came to India in 1931 to teach at a convent. She opened a school, but in no time it became a home for the dying. As she became more well-known she took on a number of Indian women as dedicated as herself. The dress adopted was one of white cotton sari with three bands of blue. On becoming even more famous she was recognised for her work by the Vatican in 1965. Her work is with the poorest of the poor, and having seen the poor of this city it is work of real significance. The foundation run by Mother Teresa now has more than 1,000 nuns. Her greatest honour among many must surely be the Nobel Peace Prize, awarded to her in 1979.

Mother Teresa was giving me her undivided attention. What a presence I was in. She is not only a Christian human being, but, - most importantly - a practising one as well. We might all think we are Christians, but how many of us put it into practice? Her Missionaries of Charity are the ultimate in Christianity. The world is a much better place for her being here. As I talked with her, she wished to know where I'd come from, what I was doing in India and where I was going. When she knew I came from England she talked of the sisters of her order in the East End of London - would I please visit them and tell them that she hoped to visit them in the near future?

We talked about the Royal family. She had great respect for them and was particularly looking forward to meeting Princess Diana, who would be visiting Calcutta in a couple of months' time. I told her I was going to visit a young lady who I'd sponsored through the charity Action Aid so she could have an education and hopefully make something of herself.

"What's her name?" she asked me.

"Albina," I answered.

"please give her my card," which she then signed. On asking my name I told her it was Brian and she signed another card with "Dear Mr Brian" on it. I told her that Albina had attended the Ursuline Convent School in Tongo, Bihar, and that I had an invitation from Sister Bernadette. I then told her that Albina was at training college, hoping to be a primary school teacher.

"You must be proud of her," she said.

"I am, very much so," I answered. My conversation with Mother Teresa went quickly. Her home for the dying destitutes is in a very noisy part of Calcutta. The noise of the traffic, with car horns blowing and music blaring away, made it very difficult for me to pick up what she was saying. She has a very soft voice. She then started pointing at my fingers. She touched each one of them and to my eternal regret, because of the noise outside, I did not hear every word. I do recall that she told me to love all people, whatever colour or race. She also mentioned other things, but again I'm afraid I couldn't catch the words.

" I have to go now," she said, "for 12 o'clock prayers." She then got up, shook my hand and joined the other sisters. I just stood there, not quite sure as to what had actually happened. This very caring and sweet old lady had gone out of her way to greet me as if I was the only person there at that particular time. That really mattered. When I came to Calcutta, just to have seen Mother Teresa would have left me satisfied, but to have been in conversation with her was spellbinding. They were five minutes I am never likely to forget. I again realised I had been in the presence of an extraordinary lady, and a very great Christian one at that.

On leaving Mother Teresa's I walked along the Lower Circular Road. I was back in the poverty and squalor. People were lying on the pavements, looking as if it would not be too long before they were taken to Mother Teresa's themselves. Some of these people just lie amidst the filth with a tin bowl at their side hoping someone will take pity on them and throw a Rupee in the bowl. Another thing I've noticed repeatedly since being in India is the seemingly extraordinary number of people who walk with a limp. Are these people deformed at birth? I'd read that babies have their legs deliberately twisted or are even blinded and put on the streets to gain sympathy from passers-by in the hope that money will be given. If this is true, it's too horrible to contemplate. Mother Teresa's home for the dying destitutes is right in the slums of Calcutta. She only has to step out of her home to see these people lying about everywhere. These beggars, unless people take pity on them, will die in the streets. Nothing is more certain.

While still walking along the Lower Circular I heard a voice say "you saw her, sir". I turned round and it was the young boy who had urged me to knock on Mother Teresa's door.

"Yes, thank you," I said. I knew that he now wanted some form of payment. The boy then told me his name was Richard and that he hadn't long to live. He told me he was dying of malaria.

"Would you like a Coke?" I asked.

"No, I only drink beer," he answered. I quickly realised I had a sharp one here. I gave him some Rupees and was on my way again. Back along the Nehru Road, who should I bump into but those children again. The young brother and sister had been waiting for me. This time there were a dozen of them. They looked dirtier than ever. I proceeded to one of the many roadside stalls and bought them a meal. This came to about £3 in English money. I sat on the pavement and just watched those kids eating as fast as they possibly could, with their fingers, of course. One girl of about 15 with her young baby also joined in. She gobbled down the food as if she couldn't believe her luck, as if someone had said 'eat it quick or it will be taken away'. These urchin kids, not one of them over eight years of age, apart from the young mother, were happy, laughing and infectious children. After the meal they climbed all over me. I must have looked as filthy as them. The whole thing must have looked hilarious and extraordinary to any passer-by, and believe me I was being watched by hundreds of Indians as these kids rolled over me. I must have looked like the eccentric Englishman Abroad. I remember taking individual photogrpahs of all the children just to show people back home. What lovely-looking kids there are in the slums of Calcutta. I got up to leave and I was followed by these children. I felt like the Pied Piper of Hamelin. I would never get rid of them now, I thought. They had even followed me to my hotel the previous evening, so they knew where to find me. They now began jumping on my back, with the better off Bengali Indians looking on in amazement. In the short time I've been here I've noticed how the people of the middle castes and, even more so, the upper castes of India look down on the poor. These poor beggars, particularly the children, seem to be a nuisance and an embarrassment to the affluent Indian. I had noticed how they spoke down to the poor. These upper and middle castes must be part of the reason why Calcutta is called Snob City. Can you imagine, amidst all this squalor, this city is called Snob City. The Calcutta high life consists of women in expensive saris and jewellery, with extreme wealth, golf clubs, polo and tennis. The poor have been exploited to the benefit of the rich. What must the poor think as they gaze through the iron gates and fences of the Calcutta Racing Club and see the higher castes at play? Thank God for Mother Teresa. She is on the side of the poor. At least someone is in this incredible city.

I deliberately lost the children after three hours of them following me. I had to tell them they couldn't keep following me. I bought them an ice cream and ran. I ran for a few minutes and when I thought I'd lost them I slowed down to a walk, hardly feeling pleased with myself. I then heard a shout. I turned round and there were the brother and sister I'd first befriended three days ago. I'd run fast and I didn't think they could possibly have kept up with me. I then spoke to them very firmly. I said I was leaving Calcutta and that I just had to leave them. The little girl who had held my hand so tightly during the day looked on the point of crying. I walked away from them. Out of guilt, I turned round and waved. I saw two of the saddest-looking children I shall ever see in my life. At that moment I could so easily have picked them up, taken them to my home in Market Deeping and adopted them. Although of course I knew it wasn't possible, with an English education they could make something of themselves. Here they had nothing. I shall think of those poor, pathetic-looking kids this Christmas as I eat my leg of turkey. Or will I be able to eat as I think of them? I felt so guilty about leaving them. What, pray God, will become of them? I certainly wasn't proud of myself. I'd made friends with the saddest, happiest, filthiest and loveliest-looking kids imaginable. I'd won their friendship and now I'd left them and felt guilty about it. Back at my hotel I couldn't get those children out of my mind. How would they survive? I felt so close to them. I said previously in this diary 'accept Calcutta for what it is and Calcutta will accept you'. Well, this is true. But it has affected me. I've never seen such poverty. Unbelievable is the only way to describe it. I don't know whether it's because I'm older in life, but I shall remember Calcutta forever. When I was 19 I did my National Service in Hong Kong and Singapore and there was poverty not unlike what I've seen here, but I was younger then and people dying in the streets did not have the effect on me that is has now. The older I get, the harder it is to believe that things like poverty exist on such a massive scale. It exists alright. To see undernourished kids, and there are countless of them in India, is not a pretty sight. I had to come to Calcutta to see it, and see it I have. And I shall never forget it.

After a lovely hot shower to rid me of even more filth I sit down to write my notes. Tomorrow I fly to Ranchi to meet Albina Kujur. Reception has just rung me to say that the flight tomorrow is to be at 11.15am and not 6.15am, so there is no need for an early call. Tomorrow should answer some questions. Is Albina married? If not, why not, because most marriages in India are arranged. What has happened to her left arm? She told me in her last letter that she had had an accident and could hardly lift her arm. I first wrote to Albina in 1978. My ambition had always been to meet her. It's taken a long time, considering also that I'd lost contact with her for nearly three years. During that time I began to think that we would never ever meet. But meet we would and tomorrow's the day. I look forward to meeting her and I know she feels the same way. I'm just curious as to what she looks like. It's about eight years since I received the last photograph and people can change over the years. Surprisingly I'm beginning to feel nervous. Tomorrow promises to be quite a day.

Day Eight   15.11.91

Hello Albina, Greetings Papa

Every morning this week at the breakfast table I've opened the morning newspaper to read about the continued violence in Bihar. People are being murdered, ambushes being set and gangs are openly creating terror in this most corrupt of all Indian states - and the one I shall be flying to today. On reading of these killings I go to Bihar with some apprehension. Bihar is known as bandit country. The state elections are on. Gangs openly go around killing who they choose. Often polling stations are blown up. They are nothing other than criminals, the paper says. Hiding behind the face of politics and politicians, these swaggering, gum-chewing, gun-slinging gangsters are getting a free hand by all accounts. Their notoriety extends throughout Bihar. One of the gang leaders freely boasts: "What can the police do to me? In my area I am the law". In other words, arrest me if you dare.

The chief minister of Bihar has a bodyguard, who is known as one of the most dreaded criminals in the state. He sits with his gang on political platforms while the chief minister speaks. With their coats undone and their guns showing they give a picture of what the old Wild West must have been like. With their Mexican-style moutaches they spread fear wherever they go. I quote from the Telegraph newspaper, Calcutta, 13 November 1991: "Terror and violence more than anything else have become the staple of political parties in Bihar. More often than not the stakes are decided by who has the bigger criminal on his side." A senior police officer then goes on to say: "Earlier it was a case of criminalisation of politics, but what is happening now can only be called the politicisation of criminals. Every party has its quota and senior leaders have begun to parade about with these elements so openly that it is extremely difficult for the law to even get near them."

The police have a terrible reputation in Bihar. Often when people are arrested they are tortured in custody and never seen again. Atrocities are commonplace. The state is a law unto itself. Can you imagine, therefore, the poor Indian factory worker in the towns and cities or the poor peasant farmer in the countryside with his nose at the end of a gun. He can't argue and he does what he's told. Nobody dare challenge the gunman. The police stand aside. They know what's going on and do nothing. The gangsters are winning, they know it and their arrogance is beyond belief. This, then is the state I go to today. I go with trepidation, but today's the day I meet Albina and there's no changing my mind now.

I write having just boarded the aircraft for Ranchi. I left the Kenelworth Hotel at 9.30am. I managed to change a traveller's cheque for Rupees at the airport - my money is lasting well. Why is it that every time I walk up the steps to a 'plane I feel under sentence of death? It's a big Indian aircraft, only a third full with probably 100 people on board. This was the flight I had least looked forward to. Would I be denied seeing Albina at the last, having come all this way? Would this 'plane fall at the final hurdle? I can't help thinking that an Indian aircraft took off from this airport only a month ago and crashed in Bangladesh with no survivors. Those poor souls would have been - like me - waiting to take off, not knowing they were minutes from death. I am, again, entirely in God's hands.

The aircraft has taken off from Dum Dum Airport. The time is 12.15. The 'plane turns to its left and as it climbs over Calcutta I look down on this sprawling city of millions, and what a city. How many people can say, having seen Calcutta, that they actually liked the place? Well, I did. I can see the Haora Bridge, also the other partially completed bridge. I can see other landmarks, like churches and large buildings - I can even see Eden Gardens. So long, Calcutta, I wouldn't have missed you for anything. Whoever said Calcutta had a soul was so very right. Amidst the rust and corrosion of a rundown city I found laughter never far away. The quite amazing thing about Calcutta is that if you ask any of its people about living anywhere else they'll say 'no way', they couldn't possibly live anywhere else. It's their city, filth and all. Once visitors like me come to terms with the most gigantic slum ever, they can actually enjoy the place. As the 'plane speeds away into the sky I also think of those children - what will happen to them? God only knows. Those scruffy, dirty urchins will be in my thoughts for months to come. They were all part of the degradation of the city. I shall remember Calcutta with affection and I shall remember it forever. I can pay it no greater compliment than to say that I would love to visit it again.

The aircraft has now started its descent into Ranchi Airport, 35 minutes after leaving Calcutta. Lots of thoughts are going through my mind. Is this state of Bihar, the most backward of all Indian states, really as violent as I've been reading? Well, I might soon find out. I think of my wife Kathleen at this time. I've been writing cards every day. I do hope she is receiving them. I know she'll be thinking of me this very day, this special day when I finally meet Albina. After all those years of writing to her my ambition of meeting her is about to be fulfilled. To achieve an ambition in life is gratifying. I was about to achieve one.

The aircraft has landed. I look out of the small window and see people waving on the airport roof. This is a very small airport. I walk down the stairway and into the sunshine. As I walk to the airport building I believe I can see them. I can spot a nun on the airport roof - it must be Sister Bernadette Tete. I can also see Albina standing next to her. She is wearing a white sari. As I walk into the building I notice they are leaving the roof to come down to greet me. I walk through the large airport doors, give my 'plane ticket to the checker, look up and there they are. Both have big smiles on their faces as I walk over to them.

I glance at Albina, but out of courtesy I first shake hands with Sister Bernadette, who is Indian and very small and proceeds to put a garland of flowers round my neck. Then I look at this girl I've never seen. It was a great moment, one to cherish. She puts her hands together in front of her face, as greetings are performed in this country.

"Greetings, papa," she says. She then also puts a garland of flowers round my neck. She is very small, petite and pretty. She has a lovely smile and seems to have an equally nice disposition. I feel a lucky man and I know my stay with her will be a happy one. I have travelled over 5,000 miles just to meet Albina and I have finally met her.

Outside the airport building we make our way to a jeep standing in the car park. Albina wanted to carry my rather heavy suitcase. As women do a lot of the work in India it was quite a natural thing for her to want to do, but I wouldn't let her. Out in the sun she looked smaller than ever, and slightly frail, I thought. At the jeep I'm introduced to Sister Albina and the driver, Sebastian. Into the jeep I go, but Sister Bernadette insists I sit in the front seat. The drive to Ranchi is only a few minutes from the airport. I get lots of looks from the people in the streets. I suppose they were curious as to who on earth this white man with all these garlands round his neck was.

Ranchi doesn't really give the impression of being a large town. Compare it to New Delhi and Calcutta and it's small, but like everywhere else I've been in India it's crowded with people. Where do they all come from, I ask myself repeatedly, these thousands and thousands of people. I thought I might have left the poverty behind in Calcutta, but there's no change. The beggars are here just the same and the sacred cow roams majestically through the streets. After about ten minutes' drive we arrive at the Ranchi Ursuline Convent School, this being the mother convent of Bihar - headquarters, so to speak. I'm introduced to a lot of the sisters who live and work here, all Indian, of course. At the lunch table I wanted very little to eat. I'd eaten on the 'plane. But the sisters were very concerned that I should eat, so rather than disappoint them I ate. Indian food it was, and very tasty, too.

At the lunch table I look at Albina, who sits opposite me. She smiles at me and I feel nine feet tall. I try to make conversation with her - all she does is smile and say "yes papa, no papa. On talking to Sister Bernadette, sitting beside me, she surprises me greatly by saying that Albina can't speak English. This really does surprise me. Over the years I'd had some lovely letters from her, first written in Hindi and then translated to English. I naturally assumed she spoke English.

Sister Bernadette said: "It's quite common for an Indian girl to write in English but be unable to speak it." No wonder, I thought, that Albina is forever smiling at me. It was her way of communicating with me. So to be told Albina could not speak English was a disappointment. Sister Bernadette told me that she will learn English in her second year at college. We would just have to communicate in some other way.

After lunch and goodbye to the sisters of Ranchi we are off in the jeep to Lohardaga, about 30 miles west of Ranchi. We travel on the roughest roads imaginable, with potholes galore - talk about being thrown about. But we eventually arrive and make for the Ursuline Training College hostel. This is where Albina is training to be a primary school teacher and where she lives. I meet even more sisters. The ones here are all teacher training sisters. I also meet Albina's teacher, who happens to come from Tongo, her pupil's home village. She tells me Albina is working hard, that she is a good girl and will hopefully make a good teacher.

I meet the principal of the college, Sister Angeline, and we have a long talk about Albina.

"She is doing extremely good work here and she has just passed an exam with a first," she tells me. "Also, Albina was so excited when she knew you were coming to see her." The principal goes on to explain that "Albina is forever studying. She probably pushes herself too hard. She has such great determination to do well, but she is so frail and wants building up." These are my sentiments exactly. I'm also told that her arm is not good. I shall hopefully see Sister Bernadette about it at the earliest opportunity.

The principal asks me if I'd like to go to the chapel evening service, which is for students. I said I would. The service having started, we creep into the rear of the chapel, which is packed with about 200 girl students. It is past 7pm, dark outside and there is very little lighting. The students have scarves over their heads. It was difficult to find where Albina was, but the principal nudged me as a voice, a Hindu voice, came out across the chapel. The principal then whispered that it was Albina and that what she said was to thank the

Almighty for bringing me from England to see her, and to thank him for what I'd done for her. After the service it was time for dinner. It was Indian food, I was hungry and I ate it - although I wasn't quite sure what I was eating. The sisters eat rice, loads of it. I fill up my plate with potatoes. Those spices really are hot. I never thought I could possibly eat Indian food, but I did and I enjoyed it.

This evening I've been in deep conversation with the college principal again. We drift into politics. She insists that Saddam Hussein is not evil, but that by taking Kuwait he was committing an evil act. She is an extremely interesting lady. I ask her about the violence in Bihar.

"It's mostly in the north," she says, "Patna, the capital of Bihar, is a violent place and terrible crimes have been committed in the surrounding countryside in that area. Whole villages have been virtually wiped out. There is no law in some of these places." She adds that Ranchi is now also becoming a violent place.

"It's not safe anywhere now. Even here in Lohardaga one can sense the violence coming. We have a high brick wall all the way round the school and gates are locked at night with guards watching the place, but still people manage to get in.

"We had a nasty experience of this recently. Burglars somehow got in one night and ravaged the place. Do you know that while the place was being burgled I had a gun pressed at my throat. One wrong move and I'd have been dead.

"The road from here to Ranchi at night is no longer a safe road to travel on."

I could see from my conversation with the principal that she was extremely worried.

"It's spreading all over Bihar, this violence. Lohardaga was once a peaceful place - not so now. It's frightening, really," she says.

Lohardaga looked to me like a small town of about 20,000 people. Surely something could be done to curb this growing violence, I thought. These poor helpless sisters in the Lohardaga convent would be at the mercy of thugs who raided the place. I went to my room with the violence very much on my mind.

I'm now completing the day's notes. It had been another eventful day, meeting Albina after all those years of writing to her of course being the highlight. But it makes me shudder to think what could happen to her and all the girl students here if these Bihar thugs run riot. Innocent girls need protection and although there is security here, with guards and high walls etc, I fear it's not enough. It's 8.55pm and lights are out by 9pm. It's going to be early to bed and early to rise during my stay of nearly two weeks in convents. I've never lived in a convent school before. It's going to be a whole new experience for me. I will have to live by the rules set by the Ursuline sisters. I am eternally grateful to them for allowing me the privilege of living with them.

Day Nine   16.11.91

I Meet The Divine Sisters of Tongo

I am up at 6am after an absolutely terrible night's sleep. The fun fair has been at Lohardaga for three days and music seemed to be belting out all night. There's nothing worse than a poor night's sleep and I've had a few since I arrived in India. I'm beginning to feel tired, though I'm sure that if I could sleep for a whole night I would feel much better. Also, my back is starting to hurt. I've had a bad back for years. I can bend down to feed the dog at home first thing in the morning and as I get up my back goes. I then have great difficulty sitting and walking. I'm only comfortable lying down. The pain is at the base of the spine. Usually it lasts for about a week, but fortunately not too often.

I thought I might be one of the first to be up and about this morning, but not so in a convent school. Before breakfast I went for a walk. I saw Sister Bernadette and she told me all the sisters are out of bed by 4.40am, with morning prayers at 6am. She then took me on a quick tour of the college. We walk by a rather large school building, where the 200 students, including Albina, are in prayer. I was shown round the classrooms and dormitories. The girls at this training college work hard. Up at 5am, they have to do various jobs like kitchen work, gardening, cleaning etc, this being done before college starts. There's no slacking here, and very little spare time. If they mean to pass exams, then it is extremely hard work. Imagine a young girl in England doing two hours of manual work before her classwork begins, working in her lunch hour, doing more work in the evening after being in class all afternoon - and trying to do homework after her evening job. It appears Albina will be here for two years. If she passes her exams she will be a primary school teacher. She then has the task of finding a teaching post. It will not be easy for her. She may have to move away from this area to find work. She could be out of work for a long period until she gets her teaching post. Also, it will certainly not be easy for a person who is now 24 years of age and who has never yet earned any money at all. But first she must pass this two-year training course before the worry of trying to find a teaching position.

After breakfast we are on our travels again, this time to my final destination, the Ursuline convent school at Tongo in the southern area of Bihar. Albina is with us - she has been given the week off college to be with me. Sister Bernadette and Sister Albina, who live at the Tongo convent school, are also in the jeep. Sebastian is a highly skilled driver. I've never been on such dreadful roads in my life. In some places there seem to be potholes every few yards and I'm being thrown up and down in the front seat. I now realise why my back suddenly started being painful yesterday. This ride was causing great pain to me, but if it hadn't been for Sebastian's excellent driving it would have been much worse. At no time did he seem to have a good stretch of road to increase speed on. I wouldn't really describe the roads as anything like the ones in England - more like country lanes. I distinctly remember going over two bridges which had nearly fallen down. We had to virtually stop on them because they were in such bad need of repair. One could look through the holes in the bridge and see the drop below. The wonder is that there are not more accidents - and fatal ones at that. I was beginning to realise what was meant by Bihar being a backward state. If the roads were anything to go by, it was certainly true.

Nearing the area of Tongo I started to notice how the countryside was changing. From Ranchi to Lohardaga it was very flat land. The southern tip of Bihar in the Tongo district has sloping green hills and the land is golden. The green and golden colours combine well to give the area a beautiful landscape. I am travelling into some of the most superb countryside one could ever wish to see, with occasional mud huts sprinkled around the area - these being the homes of the locals. Men and women are also to be seen in the rice fields, cutting their rice crop.

On this journey to Tongo I now realise I'm seeing another side of India. The countryside is a part of India the tourist would rarely see and I'm seeing it right now. The masses of people are no more. All of a sudden I feel as if I'm in a different country. I'm now moving into an area that I haven't been able to read anything about. The travel books never mentioned this part of India. Try as I might I just could not find any information about this southern tip of Bihar. I seemed to be going into no-man's land, very isolated, the back of beyond, in fact. If my company, the mighty Prudential, wanted me right now, they wouldn't possibly be able to find me. At last I've escaped from their clutches. I feel I've escaped from everywhere right now. I feel I'm millions of miles away from Market Deeping. I feel I'm on a different planet. If I wanted to abscond from the Western world then this would be the place where nobody would ever find me.

After the two-hour jeep run from Lohardaga we reach the village of Tongo, and there is the convent school. So this is the place where Albina used to write those letters to me all those years ago. We pull up at the main building and I manage to crawl out of the jeep. My back's killing me. The sisters come out to greet me, handshakes and smiles. They seem very pleased to be having me stay with them. They are all Indian, of course. There are 16 Ursuline sisters here in Tongo. They seem kind, friendly people. I know instantly I am going to like it here, this also being the convent school where I would be staying for the majority of my time.

After a wash and brush up it's into the dining hall for some lunch. I have just soup and toast and some bananas. There is a thought that laughter in this world will break down any barriers - well, these sisters can laugh alright. Every time I opened my mouth to speak, they laughed. They would laugh over the simplest of things that seemed to amuse them. I can't think why they think I'm so funny. I've never been looked upon in life as a naturally humourous and witty person. Well, if they think I'm funny I don't mind. I already have a great rapport with them and I've only known them a few hours. I quickly realised that happiness is very much a part of their lives and being happy amid constant laughter is to them what happiness is. Like the sisters at Ranchi and Lohardaga, their English is quite good, but a few of them can't understand me. I remember asking one of them if she understood me, and on my finishing this little sentence she got the giggles. Sister Bernadette and the elder sisters speak near-perfect English. I never realised back home that nuns had such a sense of humour. Rightly or wrongly I imagined their lives to be all prayers and long periods of silence. Here in Tongo their laughter borders on the hilarious.

Later in the afternoon I'm being shown round the school grounds by Sister Angela and two other sisters. I speak and the giggling goes on. Young girls who are boarders at the school stare at me in amazement as if they have never seen a white man before.

"Have you had many white people visiting here?" I ask Sister Angela.

"Yes, some come," she says, "but never one like you before. These three sisters simply howl with laughter.

"Is that good or bad, then," I ask.

"Oh, good," she replies, "oh yes, very good indeed."

I'm now being taken on a tour of the school. No lessons are on because it's well into the Saturday afternoon. It is a senior and junior school for girls. There are more than 1,300 pupils. Albina attended here for many years. The buildings are of solid brick structure. Some of them, though, look as if they want money spent on them. But everywhere is clean and tidy. This convent is giving the children in the area the chance of a better life. Without this school there would be no education for them.

I've just had a pleasant evening with the sisters, all 16 of them. I think I'll get a living as a comedian when I go home. The laughter goes on. We sat down for the evening meal at 7pm. The sisters are in prayer from 6pm to 7pm. I declined the main meal, which was boiled rice and cabbage. The sisters eat with their hands. The bowls they eat their rice from are quite large. They are forever swirling the rice and cabbage round the bowl with their fingers. I can see there is an art to eating with one's hands. I think the sisters would love to see me eating rice their way so they could have another good laugh. I like my rice as a rice pudding, as we are used to it in England. I settled for toast and soup and again a couple of bananas. How was I going to manage with their food in future? I couldn't possibly eat rice their way with gravy. I couldn't eat toast for every meal, or could I? The sisters were so eager to please me. I longed, though, for good old roast beef and Yorkshire pudding, but it was not to be - certainly not here.

Sister Bernadette Tete is the headmistress of the senior school and a real character. With a twinkle in her eye, she has a dry sense of humour. After we had eaten we were talking only by candle light, because of an electricity cut. I was quickly learning that nothing works properly in Bihar. I asked Sister Bernadette what would happen if a doctor was wanted urgently, as I knew from being told during the afternoon that there wasn't one in the school or the village.

"We would go in the jeep to Gumla, which is 18 miles away, to collect him and bring him here."

I then asked her if there was a telephone here.

"We haven't got a telephone here," she replied.

"What would happen, then, if a person were taken seriously ill and it really was an emergency," I asked.

She replied: "Well, we would collect the doctor from Gumla and it would probably take an hour for him to arrive here."

"But say the doctor arrives too late?" I asked.

"Well," said Sister Bernadette, "that seriously ill person would be dead then, wouldn't they".

At 8.30pm I say goodnight to my new-found friends, whom I've christened the Divine Sisters of Tongo. Lights are out at 9 o'clock. I've got to be in bed by this time otherwise I shall be groping about in the dark trying to get into bed and under my mosquito net, which surrounds the bed. I've just thought of something - it's 37 years since I last slept under a mosquito net, that being how long it is since I was in the army in the Far East. I'm going to morning mass at the Tongo Catholic village church tomorrow at 7am. Albina had left us earlier this afternoon to go home to see her parents. She will be spending her nights with them, but she will be in church tomorrow morning and afterwards I'm going to spend the rest of the day with Albina's family. A party is being put on especially for me. It should be an interesting day.

Day Ten   17.11.91

Mahatma Gandhi's India

Up at 6.15am for 7am mass at the Tongo Catholic village church. It's less than 200 yards from the convent school, so not too far to walk. This was the first time I had taken communion at a Catholic church. I couldn't understand what was being said at the service, as it was in Hindi. It appears that to the locals in this area of Tongo, coming to church is looked upon as a day out. The church was packed. Albina was there. She is deeply religious, but she is one amongst many here. Families had come from miles around. They really do take their religion seriously in India, whatever religion it might be.

The people in this area of South Bihar are simple peasant farmers who work in the fields from morning to dusk. Often whole families work together on their little plot of land. This being November, it is the time of year for cutting the rice crop. Mothers often have their babies strapped to their backs as they hack away in the fields. Perhaps these people working on the land and living off it do in fact feel closer to God than, say, the average person from the Western world. Going to church is very much a part of their lives. They are a tribal people - India has many different tribes within its bounds. The tribal name for the people of Tongo is Oron. They evidently came to this area many centuries ago.

Arranged marriages are so very much in evidence here. When children get into their teens their parents look around for suitable partners for them and approach other parents who also have teenage children. A deal is done and marriage arranged. I might add that arranged marriages work - no divorce here, very few separations either. To these people marriage is sacred and not to be taken lightly. Because of their strong religious beliefs, couples do stay together. They marry, have lots of children and are reasonably happy with each other. It has got me thinking that we may have got our priorities wrong in the Western world, where life so often seems to be based on greed and selfishness - 'I'm alright, Jack' and blow the others. These people here seem to be, surprisingly enough, a contented lot. I'm not saying they would not like more of a better life than they already have. Because of their hard life in the fields and carting their rice crop many miles - on foot, I might add - to hopefully sell in markets, they are in old age by the time they are 40 - so hard do they work.

Working the fields, often under a boiling hot sun, takes its toll. If their little plot of land, which they probably rent off some unscrupulous landlord, doesn't produce the vegetables, they starve. That is a simple fact. There is no unemployment money here. If the annual Monsoon is not good, nothing will grow. If I have given the impression of the Indian peasant farmer as seemingly contented, it's propably because they know no other life. This is the life that Mahatma Gandhi, who was assassinated in 1948, spoke of. Gandhi believed the real India lay in the villages. He liked the simplicity of village life. He preached the message of peace and non-violence and saw village dwellers as simple people incapable of violence as seen in the big cities. This, then, is the life that Albina was born into and brought up in. The people of Tongo were descendents of the original Indian Aborigines, who, hundreds of years before Gandhi was born, hunted with bow and arrow - and where a white-faced Westerner would fear to tread.

The jeep was ready to leave at 9.30am for Albina's home. It was draped with flowers and flags, apparently for my benefit. After the church service Albina had stayed with me. Also on the jeep were three sisters from the convent, Sister Sushila, Sister Alphonsa and Sister Albina. Sebastian the driver took the jeep down many winding lanes. The journey was only about five miles. This would be the way Albina would walk from her home to the convent school for many years. Evidently it's nothing for little children to walk five miles to school in these country areas. As we approached the area where Albina's home is, excited children were more numerous as the jeep drew nearer. Albina, who was in the jeep with me, had an excited look on her face. Something was going to happen alright. The jeep climbed a small hill and there before my eyes was the most colourfully draped house one could wish to see - flags, flowers and messages of welcome everywhere, and about 50 excitable people, who out of curiosity had gathered outside the house to see this man from England. To Albina's mother and father it was probably the biggest day in their lives. I only hoped they would be pleased with what they saw and that I wouldn't disappoint them. I needn't have worried. Whoever stepped out of that jeep was sure to get a welcome, and what a welcome it was, too.

As we pulled up outside Albina's house, this excitable crowd of people gathered round the jeep. As I climbed off, the first people to greet me were Albina's mother and father. Albina's mother put a garland of flowers round my neck. She was smothering me in hugs and kisses and she was in tears. Albina's father, who was more reserved, shook hands. I then met all the family and many of their friends. I looked at Albina's home, which was made of wood and mud. Sister Sushila then told me the welcome was in appreciation for what

I'd done for Albina. I didn't feel I'd done anything special, I'd only tried to help a poor country girl in India. But to these people I'd helped one of them and this was a day for them to return what I'd done. I never thought in my wildest dreams that I'd get a welcome like this. I was led into this mud hut and sat down at a big table. I felt like the big white hope who had discovered India. I was king for the day. They were determined to make it a day I'd never forget.

As they sat me down their faces flashed those big smiles. I could do no wrong. I felt humble. Albina's mother and another Indian lady then started taking off my socks and shoes - 'what's going on?' I thought. A bowl of cold water was placed at my feet. My feet were then lifted into it by Albina's mother, who washed them. She also washed my hands. Sister Sushila then whispered to me that this was a sign of welcome. This was a new experience for me, having my feet washed. I couldn't argue with these people. I could see the look in Albina's mother's face. She was extremely proud to be washing my feet. The surprises of the day were just beginning.

I was then taken outside the hut into the forecourt and sat down at a large table, Sister Sushila, Sister Alphonsa and Sister Albina sitting either side of me. I looked up from the table to see a crowd of inquisitive people with curious faces literally staring at me. At this point I really did feel I was at the back of beyond. The dancing girls, of which Albina was one, were brought on next. There were eight of them, all friends of Albina's. They danced a series of Indian dances, which was unlike anything I'd ever seen before. I couldn't begin to try to describe an Indian dance group. A young girl of about nine years old, who was a neice of Albina's, then proceeded to dance in a most fascinating way to steal the show. Her arms and legs seemed to be coming out of all parts of her body. I was totally absorbed by this type of dancing. The dancing and singing by different groups of girls continued to about one o'clock. I was then moved into the hut again and out came the food.

I was not quite sure what food was being put in front of me. The room I was placed in was quite dark, there being no electricity, of course. I could see lots of boiled rice, vegetables, potatoes and meat. But what meat was it? Now usually I am a big meat eater, but I just didn't know what was in front of me. I asked Sister Sushila, who sat to my right, what meat it was. Even she could not clearly tell me. For some reason I began to think of rodents, rats in other words. Was this a dead rat that I was about to eat. I knew, of course, that in certain areas of India, particularly in the countryside, some village areas are overrun by rats, thousands of them. I had also read that some religions looked upon rats in the same way as the sacred cow is looked upon. They must not be harmed in any way. This, therefore was the dilemma facing me. Dare I eat rat's meat, I asked myself. At this particular moment I felt that many eyes were on me. I felt I was going to be sick before I tried it. Sister Sushila whispered again in my ear: "Eat it, Brian. If you do not they will be offended."

I was about to try and eat whatever it was in front of me when I remembered that when I first wrote to the charity Action Aid about child sponsorship they wrote back offering me Albina to sponsor. In the letter informing me of the area where Albina lived it stated that the tribe had settled there many centuries ago and that they were the original rat eaters of India. They had to eat rats to survive. All this was going through my mind as I again tried to contemplate what was on my dinner plate. I kid you not, but if that little piece of meat had moved on that plate I'm sure I would have died a thousand deaths. As I cut through the rather tough piece of meat Sister Sushila said that the meat had been so patiently cooked by Albina's mother that morning and that it was a special treat for me.

"Please eat it Brian," she said again, "You will not only offend Albina's mother but everyone else here today. So I tried. I shall never forget that meal if I live to be 100. How I wasn't sick eating it I'll never know. Rats, or whatever it was, went down. Even so, I could only manage half of it. But at least I hadn't offended them - that was the last thing I wanted to do. I would like to say, however, that it may well not have been rat's meat I was eating. But that letter from Action Aid about Albina's tribe being the original rat eaters of India had stuck in my mind and there was no dislodging it. I must admit, though, the taste of that meat was different to any other meat I've ever eaten.

After the meal I was taken out into the forecourt again in front of a large group of people from the Tongo village. Albina's father made a speech, Sister Sushila acting as interpreter. Not speaking the local language, I hadn't any idea what he was talking about. Albina's father had said that he welcomed me to his home and said how grateful his family were for what I'd done for his daughter. They would never forget me, he said. I thanked him and his wife for their wonderful hospitality and said I would remember today forever. I then mentioned Albina and the close friendship forged over many years through writing to each other. I'd always wanted to come to India to meet her and I was finally here, but I couldn't quite believe it was all happening. As I was making this speech, which Sister Sushila was translating, I had my arm round Albina, who was so small that she barely came up to my shoulders. Although I could not communicate too well with her I felt a certain closeness to her which a man has for his daughter. A bond had been formed between us which hopefully will never die. She looked so happy to be near me and I felt so very proud to be with her.

Albina's family consists of her mother and father, four brothers and a sister. The sister is married and lives in New Delhi. All were here today with their wives and children, apart from the sister, who was just not able to travel hundreds of miles for a party, however much she wanted to, and one of the brothers, who is a student at Ranchi. The other three brothers work on the land just like their father and his father before him. I can imagine life today in these villages hasn't altered much over the years. I can see that the scene I've seen today, with little huts scattered all over the countryside, is exactly the same as the scene of 100 years ago. Nothing would have changed. Mud huts, rice, the land, the large families, arranged marriages - really a primitive life, but basically a happy and contented life. These village people have more going for them than the city people of India. At least every person here seems to get a job of sorts working on the land. In the country areas there are no beggars and one just does not see the appalling poverty here that one sees in the cities.

These people are very small in stature. I seem to tower over them. I must seem huge to them. They seem a very simple people, a very gentle people - and they are part of the lower caste system of India. I do not like this caste system. Talk about shades of discrimination - it's all here. There are 52 per cent of the entire Indian population in the lower castes. Not quite spat upon like the Dalits, known as the Untouchables - in other words the lowest of the low - the lower castes really are what Mahatma Gandhi hoped the real India would build from. I felt honoured to be in their presence. They are a very humble people and a very religious people, whose daily prayer to God would be 'please let it rain, please let the sun shine so that we can live and survive from our land.' That's what they want from life. Given those things they are therefore a contented people, and from what I've seen today a very happy people.

I look at these people's lives and then at my own. What a difference. I also look from these people's lives to the peoples of the Western world. This contentment they have, why can't it be seen in the West? The Western world is supposed to be, dare I say it, more educated and perhaps more civilised. These Indian farm workers earn a pittance, perhaps five Rupees (16p) a week, but I bet many of them are more contented with their lot than many a grasping Westerner is. Progress is a fine thing. These people's lives have progressed hardly at all over the centuries, unlike, say, the Western world. But are we in the West any happier for this progress? Looking at these tribal people today they do not have much to be happy about. Albina's parents look much older than me, but they could be years younger. Their hard life has taken its toll on them. The average Indian dies at around the age of 50, usually from starvation in the cities and exhaustion in the country areas. I've seen such love and happiness here today. They are not envious of people in the West because they do not know any other life. If God looks after them with the rain and sun then their prayers are answered, this being the reason why the church was overflowing with these people this morning. Life to them is simple, they seem to have their priorities right. Can we in the West learn something from these tribal people in deepest India? I leave you to your own conclusions on that.

The afternoon was generally spent talking through one of the sisters, who acted as an interpreter to different members of Albina's family. I was shown round the mud hut which to these people is home. It's built of wood and mud. How these places are not swept away by the excessive Monsoon rains when they come I'll never know. But these homes are clean inside. The Indians are generally a clean race, forever washing themselves and cleaning their teeth. Their teeth are cleaned by a sprig of wood from a tree, this being their toothbrush. This sprig of wood has the desired effect because all Indians have dazzling white teeth. Albina, with her snow-white teeth, chocolate-coloured skin and long, jet-black hair tied at the back, is an attractive-looking girl. But, like I found in the slums of Calcutta, many of the women have stunning good looks. Take Victoria, Albina's best friend. She really is a lovely looking girl. When looks were given out this girl was in the top drawer, with her shining ebony skin, high cheek bones and classic features she is a genuine beauty - and I say that in the nicest possible way. She is so striking she ought to be in Indian films. She wouldn't be out of place with her face on the cover of Vogue magazine. I just cannot get over the fact that India is a country of good looking women, and the most beautiful are often to be found in the unlikeliest places. But because they are so poor and humble many do not realise how good looking they are. There is no vanity or arrogance about them. Here in the lower caste system of India a woman knows her place in life. Any form of vanity would be frowned upon. The husband is very much the head of his family. His wife knows her status in life - to obey her husband, work hard (in many cases harder than her husband) have lots of children, and all of this uncomplainingly.

Looking over Albina's parents' home, there weren't any beds, just blankets laid out - no mod cons here, everything so basic. I was shown to the well at the rear of the hut. Ordinary rain water would be drunk by all the village with the strange food they eat, strange that is to us in the West, where one would think of tummy upsets. Talking of drink, I tasted the very popular homemade rice beer. I'm not sure what the ingredients were, but several members of the family were well gone on this drink. Some started to sing Indian songs. They were extremely happy. I did try this drink, but it did nothing for me. Rice with water, or whatever, tasted very ordinary, but these village people thrived on it. Mugs were forever being topped up. It crossed my mind what they might think of the West's intoxicating liquor. One sip of strong beer and they would be asleep. But they were happy - laughter was certainly in Albina's home today. I really had been to deepest India. I refer again to Mahatma Gandhi. His famous prediction was that "the future of India will be settled in the villages and not in the big cities." He loved the simplicity of village life and he campaigned tirelessly against the caste system. Although he was born into the comfortable middle caste, he realised the unfairness of caste. I've today been with the lower castes. If Gandhi really did like the simplicity of village life, then I had found it. These simple people, these descendents from the tribe of Oron, lived a simple life. These tribal people wouldn't know what violence was. Gandhi had seen this in the countryside himself and I knew what he had meant. I had seen it myself.

At 5pm we left Albina's home to return to the convent. All the family came over to hug me. This was goodbye and thank-you. Albina's mother didn't want me to go. She was in tears again. This woman was completely overwhelmed by my visit. The jeep then started its short journey back to the convent school. My final memory of Albina's family is of about 30 of them waving furiously as our jeep disappeared from their sight. Little Ambrose, Albina's four-year-old nephew who had sat on my knee all afternoon, ran after the jeep. His father quickly picked him up. It had been an extraordinary day, certainly it was another day spent in India that I would never forget.

Back at the convent the sisters wanted to know of the day's happenings. We discussed Albina's family and all the peasant farmers throughout India. I was told that as they knew of no other life they were reasonably contented. After supper I go to my room. It's soon 9 o'clock and lights out. I climb under my mosquito net and think of rats and my stomach. No after effects yet, I thought. I laugh myself to sleep. Could I really have eaten rat's meat? I'll never know what it was. But I'd survived. Tomorrow I'm to get a welcome from the whole school, so it promises to be another eventful day.

Day Eleven 18.11.91

Hearty Welcomes

On walking by the notice board in the dining room this morning I noticed that 'Hearty Welcomes' was written on it in big block capital letters, this being the sisters' way of greeting me. If I thought yesterday's welcome by Albina's family was something very special then today's welcome by the whole of this Ursuline convent school of Tongo was nearly as good.

After breakfast Sister Bernadette took me on a conducted tour of the whole school. It is divided into senior and junior schools. Going through the senior school first, all the classrooms were empty, not a pupil to be seen anywhere. I asked Sister Bernadette where everybody was - everywhere was so very quiet.

"Where are the children," I asked her.

"You will see them soon," she said. The classrooms were large brick buildings and quite impressive. They were well built, which rather surprised me, although I wasn't sure what to expect. Perhaps I expected the classrooms to be mud huts, after all most of the buildings in the Indian countryside are built of mud and wood. But I was impressed, and looking over the classrooms one could have been looking over an English classroom. Chairs and desks seemed to be in good condition. These Indian children here were not going without anything in these classrooms and I'm sure they could only be happy here.

On coming out of the last classroom and into a corridor we turned right and into the playground to be greeted by about 700 pupils. All the senior school was here. Spontaneous clapping broke out and this went on for a few seconds. They were clapping furiously, such happy, laughing children in their school uniforms. I wasn't prepared for a reception like this. All the Ursuline sisters of Tongo were also here. Sister Bernadette was laughing. She hadn't let on. I was looking into a mass of coloured faces. The head girl then gave greetings in Hindi and I was garlanded with flowers. I was then told to sit and the whole of the senior school then proceeded to sing some Indian songs. I had never given it a thought that "hearty welcomes", as is often said in Indian greetings, would be like this.

Sister Bernadette then spoke, saying that I had come from England to visit the school and see a young lady, Albina Kujur, who he had sponsored through the charity Action Aid, to attend the school. I was beginning to feel quite embarrassed by what she was saying. Her message was translated to me in English. In reply I thanked everyone here for their glorious welcome. I did say that because Albina had studied hard at this school she was now training to become a teacher. Work hard and one day you can hopefully be where Albina is, I said. I then took my camera from my pocket and proceeded to take numerous photos of them. They were deliriously happy. Indian children love to be photographed. They were happy enough before. Now they were hysterical in their laughter.

I was then directed by Sister Bernadette to the junior school area. Again, I was being taken round the classrooms, this time by the junior school headmistress, Sister Scholastica. I was just as impressed with the classrooms. I was taken into the junior school playground and there they were again, only this time it was the junior pupils. On greeting me, Sister Scholastica said about the same as Sister Bernadette had said. There are 600 pupils here in the junior school. The clapping continued. If anything, the juniors were more excited than the seniors. Talk about hearty welcomes - I was completely overwhelmed by it. After about an hour with the junior school I was taken by Sister Bernadette to the school hall. By now I was overloaded with garlands. The school hall is the other side of the playground. On making this short walk of around 300 yards, about 200 pupils followed me. On approaching the school hall Albina was there to greet me and so I was directed inside. I sat down to be greeted by Indian music and dancing - the hall was full of schoolchildren. I was by now becoming totally fascinated by Indian dancing. These schoolchildren love music and dancing, certainly not Western-style, though. They wore saris of many colours. They were putting on this extraordinary show for me. How could I ever thank them?

This music and dancing went on for about an hour. Sister Bernadette again stood up to give greetings. I then said in reply how I'd enjoyed this Indian dancing. What possessed me I'll never know, but I then proceeded to demonstrate the Twist on the school platform in front of hundreds of Indian schoolchildren. Now these Indian country children had, in all probability, never seen any Western-style dancing. Well, I tried my best with the Twist. The children screamed with delight. They had seen nothing like this before. My poor imitation of the Twist sent them wild with delight. Probably because of making a fool of myself I felt I was being accepted by them. I had broken a barrier. I would now be able to mix with them and talk to them. This meant a lot to me. I had won these school kids over. I wanted their confidence and I believe I'd got it.

Celebrations at last over and back to the main building for lunch, where I sat down once more at this big long table with the 16 sisters. They had their usual rice. Dove and chips was cooked for me and it tasted really good. The sisters were beginning to put on special meals for me. They knew I just couldn't eat their rice. I was very appreciative - they were bending over backwards trying to help with English-style food. I knew I was in very good hands. Laughter was never far away. They were happy, the schoolchildren were certainly happy and I definitely was. This was the holiday of a lifetime. What memories I have of India. I wouldn't miss what I've seen and experienced for anything.

Lunch over, Sister Bernadette took me halfway around the compound brick wall. This wall stretches about one mile round the whole of the convent school. Sister Bernadette explained that because of thefts by some local people scaling the wall and stealing vegetables from the school gardens, and also some valuables from inside the convent, the wall has had to be raised to eight feet in some areas to keep out undesirables. This has cost a lot of money. She has written begging letters to various people and organisations asking for help, but the money has now stopped coming in. There is still a lot of the wall to be completed - parts of it have been completely knocked down. Could I help, she asks, as nearly £3000 in English money would finish the job. I said I would try to help. I'm not quite sure if I can, though. I did at least tell her I would try.

This afternoon I was taken with Albina and her friend Victoria, along with Sister Bernadette and Sister Sushila, to Chainpur College, about half an hour's run in the jeep. This is the college Albina went to when she left the convent school. She attended here for two and a half years. She lived at this college and was doing very well, training to be a schoolteacher. But because of some government disturbances the college closed some six months ago and has not re-opened since. I understand 200 students attended here. Several of them were hanging about the place with their books at the ready hoping that somehow the college would open up again. What a shame, I thought. These kids have it hard enough without disturbances, strikes or whatever to disrupt their lives. Albina had been extremely fortunate. Sister Bernadette had arranged for her to complete her studies in the Lohardaga convent training school. But Albina's friend Victoria was not so lucky. She was just hoping that the college would soon open again. I'm quickly learning that what is being said about the Bihar government - that it is a shambles, that all the politicians seem to do is argue and talk party politics - is true. I wish they would put the future of India first, because It's these youngsters who are the future and desperate to learn and educate themselves for the benefit of their country. Bihar is a strike-riddled state. Does anything work properly here? From what I've seen it does not - and that is certainly to the detriment of the children.

Sister Sushila wanted to take me to her home to meet her parents, who lived in the village of Chainpur. So, after five minutes' drive in the jeep we pulled up at a mud hut. All the homes are mud huts. It would have done Western eyes good to have seen that poor home. No lights, no carpets, very scant furniture, but clean as can possibly be, considering the cattle. Yes, I repeat, cattle. They were driven through the home twice a day. Sister Sushila's father owns six cattle, a cow and five goats. Every morning the cattle are taken to graze in the fields and the only way for them to get from the rear of Sister Sushila's home, where they are kept in a shed, to the fields is through the home - through the front door, in fact, often dropping cow dung on the way. Can we in the Western world imagine cattle walking through our living rooms twice a day? But I'm beginning to realise that these peasant farmers do not know any different and because of that they just get on with their lives. As at Albina's home I was struck by the contentment of these Indian country folk. I'd had a lovely welcome into that home and Sister Sushila was so proud to introduce me to her parents.

We arrived back at the Tongo convent school for five o'clock, having dropped Albina and Victoria off in Tongo village for them to go home. I have started writing my diary for the day. I must get as much done in daylight as possible. Nightfall here comes at six o'clock. Every evening the electricity is switched off - more disruptions by this Bihar government. What they are proving I don't know. This convent has its own generator, though, which produces electricity. It runs every evening from 7pm to 9pm, but even then the light is not good. The sisters, though, all seem to accept these happenings as very much a part of their lives. They do not grumble. I just wish, though, that the officials or politicians, or whoever is running Bihar, could see the very trying conditions the sisters are living under. But these Ursuline sisters of Tongo are the uncomplaining type. Far be it for them to grumble, that is not their style. Life here can be very primitive indeed, what with the electricity cuts, water pipes leaking all over the convent school, no hot water baths and showers not working either. As I'm finishing my notes just before going down to supper, Sister Sushila brings me a bucket of warm water for me to wash myself down. What would I do without Sister Sushila. She is an angel to me.

At supper this evening, Sister Vianney pours soup into my bowl, or I should say tries to. While talking to someone else, she proceeds, accidentally, of course, to pour the boiling hot soup into my lap. I nearly jumped through the ceiling. Instead of sympathy, however, all I got was howls of laughter. Whatever misfortune befalls me, these sisters can see the funny side. They really have a wicked sense of humour. Fortunately the soup didn't penetrate too far through my trousers. The same Sister Vianney then knocks a cup of tea flying, luckily not in my direction. Talk about laugh. I looked round the table this evening, and this convent school in Bihar must be the happiest place in India. It's certainly the happiest place I've ever stayed at. Not so funny, though, is my back. Several times today I could hardly bend down. If my wife were with me she would be rubbing ointment into it. But she is not here. Perhaps one of the sisters will rub ointment onto my back. I can imagine the laughs that will get, with my trousers half down while one of them massages my back. Will I offend them, I ask myself. Afterall, these are not ordinary people as such. Will they be embarrassed? I'll have to ask Sister Bernadette. I'm on such good terms with all of them that I'm certain I won't offend them. I'll have to do something - I can hardly climb into bed. Oh, what I'd give for a hot bath.

Mahatma Gandhi's memorial in New Delhi

New Delhi bus - packed in like sardines they are

In the streets of Calcutta, bustees are what the people live in on the left

Fatehpur Sikri is a deserted city, built of red stone, the author with the five tiered Panch Mahal in the background

The authors little friends, the street kids of Calcutta

This time eating a meal I'd bought them

Early morning wash for some in Calcutta

The sacred cow at Ranchi all four of them

Mother Teresa, the great christian, I had to pinch myself says the author, because
I was in the company of an extraordinary presence. My thanks to MASU for this
photograph

The door to Mother Teresa's orthanage

Mother Teresa's message to Mr Brian

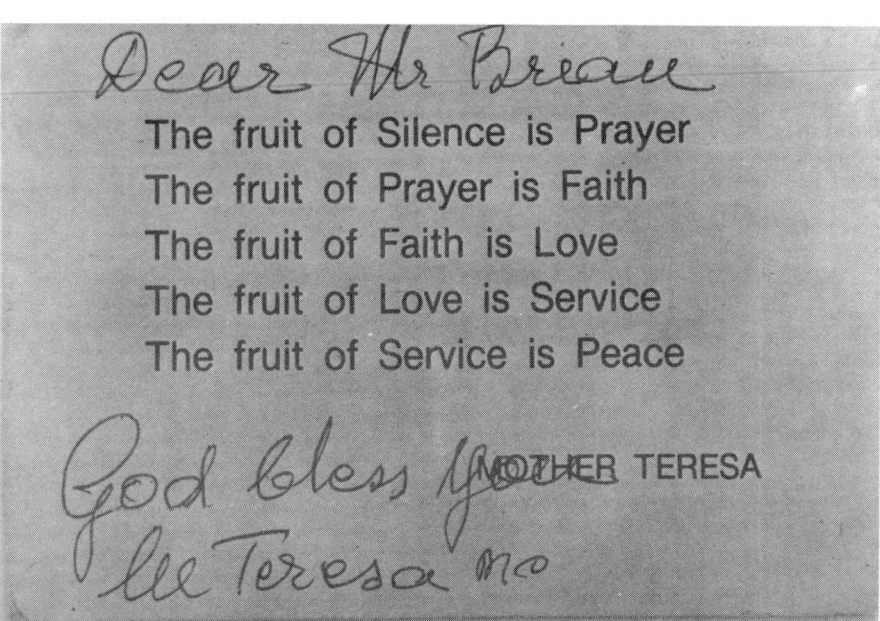

Dear Mr Brian

The fruit of Silence is Prayer
The fruit of Prayer is Faith
The fruit of Faith is Love
The fruit of Love is Service
The fruit of Service is Peace

God bless you MOTHER TERESA
Me Teresa mc

The author stands on hallowed turf, the magnificent Eden Gardens cricket ground, where 95,000 people watched a one day international just two days before

More flowers, the author being welcomed by the High School girl's at Tongo

The author being greeted and garlanded by Albina's family on arrival at their home

The author with Albina, when he met her it was the realization of a dream

The author with Albina and her parents

The author having his feet washed, this was Albina's mother's way of welcome for me to their humble home

One white face

Such happy children this photo is of the juniors

A group of the school juniors on arrival at school, some of these children had walked many miles to get there from the Indian countryside

This photograph of the jeep I travelled in, left to right: Sister Michael, Sabastian, Victoria, Albina, Ambrose, Sister Sushila, Sister Scholastico and Albina's brother

The countryside of Tongo, this road lead's to the Tongo covent school

Morning mass in the countryside of Tongo

Sister Bernadette Tete who invited me to Tongo, with Sister Vianney

The author with fourteen of the Divine sisters of Tongo, there official name being the Ursuline Sisters of Bihar

The author cuts the cake for his last supper in Tongo, made especially for him

Day Twelve   19.11.91

Back Troubles and a Mission

Couldn't sleep last night, not just because of my back, which was giving me so much pain that I could hardly turn over in bed, but because I began to think that this convent was overrun by rats. Strange scratching noises in the night, also human noises like moans and groans - or is ghosts at work? Ghosts in a convent school, I thought. Well, it could happen. Ghosts are just as likely to be walking around here as anywhere else. It depends if one believes in ghosts. Until I see ghosts, I for one will not believe in them.

At breakfast I asked the sisters about the strange scratching noises. No rats here, I was told, but plenty of mice. I again had toast for beakfast. I don't think I'll ever eat toast again when I get home - not many meals here go by without it. How they enjoy their rice. I mention my back to Sister Bernadette.

"Sister Sushila will rub some ointment on your back for you," she says. So, after breakfast it's up to my room. I lie on my bed, half drop my trousers and Sister Sushila gently rubs in the ointment. What a relief, I thought.

"I bet you haven't rubbed ointment into a man's back before," I say jokingly.

"No, I haven't," she smiles. She then goes to get me a hot water bottle, which she puts under my back as I lie on my bed. I can't possibly get off the bed at present. At least lying here I'm comfortable.

Ever sworn in a convent? Well, I have. While lying on my bed I tried to move into a chair. The pain was excruciating. I'm now really beginning to think that I may have done some serious damage to my back. Unfortunately Sister Fredric, the convent nurse who runs the dispensary where the children and local people are taken when they are ill, is away for a few days at another convent. She would, of course, have been a big help to me. But alas she is not here. I will just have to grin and bear it.

Later in the morning Albina and Victoria call to take me for a walk down to the river. I've got to try to get moving, I thought. Sister Sushila, who keeps popping in to see me, tells Albina to rub ointment into my back as well. Down come my trousers again. Sister Sushila then demonstrates to Albina how it's done. Victoria is also in the bedroom. Now in come Sister Michael and Sister Josephine. The room is now full of sisters who keep looking at and probing my back. What fun they all seem to be having. I could also see the funny side, the trouble was that every time I laughed my back hurt.

After Albina had massaged my back for about half an hour I got off the bed and was able to stand. I often feel better standing when I have these back troubles, so I decided to go for this short walk with Albina and Victoria. The river is only about half a mile from the convent. Out in the fresh air and sunshine I felt better. The sun is always shining here. I take another look at the countryside. How beautiful it is. It's amixture of green and gold and rolling hills in the distance. A lot of the hills are covered in forest. I just can't get over how colourful the countryside is here.

We arrive at the river - hardly a river, though. Perhaps a deep stream would be a better way of describing it. When the Monsoon is here it is, of course, a very deep river. The excessive rains of the Monsoon not only fill the rivers, but can often flood whole areas. On crossing the river by stepping on large stones I slipped and fell in. I then swore for the second time today. What pain I was in - and I was soaked from my waist down. The two girls helped me up. Without them I think I'd still be there now. I made it to the other side, socks, shoes and shirt came off and I was soon dry again in the hot Indian sun. We walked back to the convent. I tell the sisters what has happened - they can see the funny side. How they giggle and laugh. Laughter is never far away here. Any misfortune to me and they continue to laugh.

During lunch I happen to say to the sisters how well we are all getting along. Even some of the more junior sisters can now begin to understand me, and me them. I then say: "i hope you do not think I am stupid in any way."

Sister Michael then asks: "Why do you think we think you're stupid?"

"Well I am English and different to you. I know at times it's not been easy for some of you to understand me," I say.

"Listen, Brian," says Sister Michael, "you might think we are stupid, but the important thing is that we do not think you are stupid." We all laugh. Nothing is taken too seriously here.

After lunch I go for a short stroll of about half a mile with Sister Sushila, starting at the main entrance gate. This turned out to be a most interesting conversation. She wanted to know about my life in England, which she always seemed to be asking about. I now thought it was time for me to ask the questions. We talked. about her life as a nun.

"We are all sisters here," she said.

"Any regrets?" I ask.

"Regrets none," she says. "What could be finer than serving God? I work for him. He is my life." She then told me that when she was a young girl - she would be about 40 years of age now - a marriage had been arranged by her parents. "They are all arranged marriages here," she says, "but I had a choice between marrying a nice local boy who I know would have made me a good husband or giving my life to the Lord. But my duty was to God, so I never married and I couldn't be happier. We are so happy, us sisters," she says. I must admit this Tongo Ursuline convent school was just about the happiest place I've ever been in.

"Tell me, Brian," she says, "why is it that couples in your country or any Western world country simply live together?" She couldn't understand this living together. "Why don't they get married?" she asks.

"Well," says I, "some couples live together and treat it as a trial period and when they find they are still as much in love, then they often marry."

"But they don't always marry, do they," she says.

"No," I say, "but that's their choice."

"What happens when these couples get fed up with each other and probably have no intention of getting married and split up?"

"Well, they probably find other partners," I say.

"What, intercourse again with someone else?" she asks.

"Yes," says I, "there might be intercourse with lots of partners."

She says: "I find that very sad indeed. They can't be happy, can they? It couldn't happen here.

"All that intercourse I find very sad. People marry and stay married here." She continues to shake her head as we walk back to the convent. "All that intercourse," she says again. "They can't be happy, can they?"

I am now lying on my bed with a hot water bottle under my back. I'm really annoyed. Fancy coming all this way to India and hurting my back. This was the last thing I wanted to happen. I do not wish to be a liability to the sisters here. I shan't look forward to travelling in the jeep again. Being thrown about in the jeep has obviously damaged my back. Tomorrow we take Albina back to Lohardaga Training College and then on to Ranchi. I shudder to think of those roads - potholes galore. I hope I'll be alright.

While I lie on my back in my bedroom Sister Michael brings another hot water bottle. Like Sister Sushila she really does fuss round me. Then, surprising me greatly, she goes on to say that God has sent me here on a mission.

"What do you mean?" I ask her.

"God has sent you here to see and help Albina. What you have done for that girl was a Christian act." I tell her I've done absolutely nothing. "Look at Albina's family," she says, "look at the happiness at what you have done for their Albina. You remember what I say. You have been sent here for a purpose, you have been sent here on a mission," she says again. I couldn't argue with this sweet elderly sister. It was time to go downstairs for supper and with her help I made it off the bed. Dear Sister Michael does ramble on so. What on earth was this mission she was talking about? My only mission right now was getting on and off my bed. I'm now in great pain. What have I done, I ask myself. How can I continue to enjoy my stay here while stretchered on my bed? I feel useless. I'm totally reliant on others to help me.

After supper I say goodnight to the sisters. I must lie down. My back's killing me. During supper the sisters asked me would I like a game of cards. I had to decline. Evidently card playing is the great indoor sport in this convent. I just had to lie on my bed. At least I'm comfortable there. Sister Sushila follows me into my room. I somehow manage to get on the bed and she rubs more ointment on my back. Her soft hands are pure magic. I tell her she is spoiling me with kindness.

"I do not spoil you, I love you," she replies. Well, there's no answer to that, is there. She then brings me another hot water bottle and says goodnight. After she has gone I'm able to get off the bed and do some more writing. I must keep up with the day's events. I smile to myself. I've travelled thousands of miles since I left England and here I am in the back of beyond in India and I find a woman who tells me she loves me. But these Ursuline sisters of Bihar love everybody. When Sister Sushila told me she loved me it was said with genuine affection for another human being. These are God's teachings and the sisters abide by them. I know there would never be any wars in the world if everyone had this love for each other as the sisters do. I may be unlucky with my back at present, but I also know I'm lucky to have met the Divine Sisters of Tongo. What women they are. I know I'm a liability to them right now, but in all honesty I couldn't be in better hands.

Day Thirteen   20.11.91

Lohardaga Convents

The morning bell clangs at 4.40am. It usually wakes me up because it's so loud I lie in bed for another hour or so. At 6am I can hear the sisters in prayer in the convent chapel. After prayers Sister Sushila brings me a bucket of warm water for a wash and shave. She asks how my back is. I tell her I believe it's a little better. I tell her I'm not looking forward to the trip to Lohardaga - all those potholes. Sister Sushila then tells me she will get some cushions for me to sit on in the jeep. With a hot water bottle I should be comfortable, she says.

The reason for this journey to Lohardaga is of course to take Albina back to college, and while I'm there to be shown round other convents, one of which is a hospital. The following day we are to take Albina to Ranchi hospital to see what can be done for her left arm. I would be getting a specialist's report. Her arm has been this way now for over three years. The condition was caused when she fell off a pedal cycle. She cannot lift anything with the arm and can hardly lift it waist high. The elbow bone has come out of its socket. Although she is in some pain with it, the pain is not great. Here in India in particular, if poor people have any deformity they have to live with it. As the poor cannot afford hospital treatment, many a child could be deformed all its life. In Albina's case, I was hoping that a simple operation would get her arm as good as new again. As she tries to lift her arm the bone sticks out, which is not a pretty sight. Also, she is unable to comb her hair properly. Usually a friend will do it for her.

On the journey to Lohardaga, which is about 30 miles, I saw lots of peasant farmers working their little plots of land, cutting the rice crop which will finish up in village markets. The way they walk along these country roads with the rice crop balancing on both ends of a six-foot stick across their shoulders one thinks their legs will buckle. Theirs is a hard life, and often by the time some of them are 40 they are old men. There are no overweight people in the Indian countryside. They work too hard to ever put on weight.

The cushion that Sister Sushila had placed in the jeep for me to sit on was a big help. Those potholes didn't seem half as bad. I was still relieved when we arrived at Lohardaga, though. With Sebastian the driver were Sister Bernadette, Sister Michael, Albina and myself. On arriving at the training college at Lohardaga we were again greeted by the principal, Sister Angeline. Over tea and biscuits, Sister Angeline again talks of the ever-increasing violence coming to this area. She says that in Ranchi, which is not all that far away, a security guard was shot dead yesterday. Killings seem to be regular occurences now, she says. In view of what had happened to this sister only quite recently, when a gun was pointed at her throat, I could well understand her worry. While in Calcutta I had read in the newspapers that one well-known gunman in Bihar was openly boasting that no one would stand in his way, and if it meant killing people, which he does, then so be it. The trouble, as I see it, is that the politicians are a poor lot, often protecting these known criminals. The ordinary Indian is a very gentle person, just right for these bullying thugs to pick on. I fear for the future of this state of Bihar. I can only hope and pray that the violence never comes to the Tongo area.

Later in the afternoon, Sister Michael suggests a tour of the college gardens. Albina comes with us. The time is five o'clock, school work is over and all the students are busy with their jobs. Some are tending their gardens, where they grow their own vegetables, which of course will be used to feed all the students here. Great emphasis is placed on the students being able to turn their hands to anything, from baking in the cookhouse to washing clothes, scrubbing floors and other general duties in the college. There is also cattle, two cows, lambs and chickens, which also have to be fed. It is important, and very much a part of the students' training, that all these chores have to be done. If they fail their exams they could well find themselves back in their villages - when hopefully a marriage can be arranged - having babies and living the life their parents and their parents before them have lived.

This evening I was taken in the jeep with Albina and Sister Bernadette to the Lohardaga convent hospital, which is about a mile from the training school. It seemed as much a hospital for the people of Lohardaga. Many local people were occupying the beds. It was now dark and, there being no electricity in the wards, nurses were managing with the use of torches, candles and gas lamps. I asked one of the doctors what would happen if an emergency operation was required. The doctor assured me that a generator could soon be switched on. While I was in the hospital I was introduced to a white Belgian sister, Sister Elice, who came to Bihar in 1953. As the Ursuline sisters originally came from Belgium there were of course many Belgian sisters working in India in those early years.

As the years went by the white sisters became fewer. Consequently, Sister Elice told me, only five white sisters remained in Bihar. She was a lovely lady and spoke very good English. What devotion to God, I thought. To have left one's homeland and come here to spread the word of God one must be a special person. Her heart was in India. She had obviously had the call from God to work and serve him in a foreign country. What brave women the four orginal Ursuline sisters must have been when they came to Bihar in 1903. Sister Elice had given her life to the education of Indian children. This sister was, to me, one of the unsung heriones of the world. She loved India and I'm sure she will die in India.

On leaving the hospital Sister Bernadette was very keen to show me the Lohardaga convent school, less than five minutes away by jeep. Evidently Sister Bernadette had a lot to do with the design and layout of the buildings here. At every convent I've been to I've been impressed with these brick buildings. Sister Bernadette was in charge of this convent school for many years. The convent was very dark with, again, very little lighting. The children, about 400 of them, were singing in front of the statue of Mary in the playground. It was lit up, even though there was no electricity, and it looked very impressive. Perhaps the statue lighting was controlled by batteries. What a pity, though, that there was again no power. I was being shown round as best as was possible. The sisters had torches in their hands as we went from classroom to classroom. I felt sorry for Sister Bernadette. She so wanted to show me round this school, the building of which she had obviously had so much to do with. Bihar continued to amaze me. Does electricity work properly anywhere in this state? These wonderful Ursuline sisters, whichever convent school they may teach at, are dedicated to their work. But they never grumble. They accept Bihar for what it is and get on with their work. And what placid women they are. However trying the circumstances, they accept them. God had called them to serve him and no electricity cuts were going to stop them.

Just had supper with the sisters here. Sister Bernadette has been telling the principal of the training school how well I have been received in Tongo. The principal then referred to me as the Father of Tongo, which created great laughter around the table. After supper I went to the kitchen to help with the washing up.

"You are too old to wash up. You are a grandfather," one sister said. I got hold of a cloth.

"You can tell he does it at home," another sister remarked. It's away to bed now and lights out. Tomorrow it's off to Ranchi hospital and hopefully something can be done for Albina's arm.

Day Fourteen 21.11.91

Ranchi Hospital

After breakfast, which was just after 6am, we were off by jeep to Ranchi. I was up that bit earlier because of the day ahead, with Sebastian of course the driver. Albina had permission from the principal to have another day off college. Albina also brought along a friend because she would be catching a bus back to Lohardaga later in the day. The principal had told me yesterday evening that it wouldn't be safe for a young girl to be alone on a bus. Sister Bernadette, Sister Michael and myself would be staying overnight at the Ranchi convent school. Albina's week off from college was nearly up, so when she catches the bus back to Lohardaga I shall only see her once more before my flight from Ranchi to England, which is now only a week away. Have I really been in India nearly two weeks? Doesn't time fly, I thought.

The two-and-a-half hour jeep journey to Ranchi played havoc with my back. Although I was well fitted up with hot water bottles and cushions, I wasn't really giving my back a chance to get better. How I cursed those potholes. The country roads in India have to be seen to be believed. I don't think Sebastian managed 30mph during our journey - more like 15mph on average. It's certainly a way of cutting down on vehicles speeding on these roads. With our first stop in Ranchi being the hospital, perhaps I was going to the appropriate place. I certainly had no intention of mentioning my back to anyone in any hospital. I would have to grin and bear it.

My previous look at Ranchi was when I flew in from Calcutta. Today I have seen considerably more of it. It is a small industrial town and there seemed to be plenty of chimney smoke and smog about. This very much reminded me of being in an industrial area. There are factories that are actually thriving. I was entering the heavy engineering and machine tools industry area. Not too far from here is the town of Jamshedpur, which is where the heavy steel industry begins. Also in Ranchi is the biggest mental asylum in all India. I dreaded to think what people were like in this asylum, as I had seen enough mental disorders in the streets of New Delhi and Calcutta. In those cities some people run around in a mental state. There is a university in Ranchi. The town is known as the summer capital of Bihar and was once a retreat for the British. It has a cool climate, being 700 metres above sea level.

Having said that, Ranchi is a small industrial town. It has a population of 500,000, which I suppose is relatively small in comparison to other Indian towns and cities. By Western standards, a population of this size would make Ranchi a huge city. It is packed with people. What I've noticed here, as in other cities in India, is that going to the toilet is not the private, personal thing it is in Western-style countries. To see a man urinating in any street, yes, even the main shopping areas and without even turning his back to the traffic, is quite common. I must admit, however, that finding a toilet here is not that easy. I'm not sure how the women manage. The very private act of going to the toilet is not private here, and nobody seems to care.

The usual number of rickshaws are in constant use here. Motorcycle rickshaws often have as many as eight people inside, sometimes more. By normal road safety standards they should probably hold no more than three people. But it is the pedal rickshaw puller I feel sorry for. These people are terribly thin. To earn a Rupee they might have to cycle for over two miles with their passengers. Their bodies are skin and bones, their ribs very pronounced as they strain to cycle uphill. They earn every Rupee they get with sweat.

On arriving at Ranchi we made our way to the hospital. I was keen to have Albina's left arm looked at. When we arrived at this hospital I couldn't really believe what I saw - it was absolutely filthy. Since I've been in India I've become so used to what I've seen that when I'm taken by surprise it leaves its mark. The state of that hospital was a complete surprise. I could tolerate the filth in Indian cities. I could also understand that India, being a Third World country, has terrible problems with over-population and I could understand, to a certain extent, the appalling squalor of the big cities. But what I couldn't accept was the state of this hospital. The hospital was on strike, no staff in today, we were told. Goodness knows, then, who looks after the wards.

On walking through the hospital corridors I saw the most miserable-looking dog roaming around with sores all over its filthy body. I thought of rabies. I saw gangs of youths riding on a motorcycle - this, I repeat, inside the hospital. Window ledges had months of dust on them; walls and floors looked grimy. A rust-ridden lift that didn't work looked as though it hadn't worked for years. The general look of the place was grubby and dirty in the extreme. I thought of the chairman of my cricket club, who is a local GP. What would his reaction be if he were here? I myself had the feeling that if I were ever rushed to this hospital for whatever reason, it may be that I might never come out alive. We did manage to find a doctor and his appearance did nothing to improve the place. He looked in need of a good wash himself. Albina's arm was X-rayed and we knew for sure that she had dislocated it. The waiting room where we waited was unbelievably filthy - those black walls and rubbish on the floor. What was an operating theatre like here, I thought. When will India, or should I say this attrociously governed state of Bihar, get its act together? There can never be any possible excuse for what I saw in that hospital, however poor the country may be.

When Albina dislocated her elbow over three years ago it was felt that nothing could possibly be done for her. All it required, though, was a simple operation. This may appear easy enough in England, but here it is different. Albina hadn't any money, her family certainly didn't have any either, so nothing could be done. The arm was left to heal by itself. Consequently the bone sticks out of the side of her arm and because she is unable to lift her arm above waist height it is practically useless. So tomorrow, as this hospital is on strike, we would hopefully take the X-ray to a doctor who runs a private clinic. It was no good enquiring at this hospital. There was no telling how long the strike would last and from what I'd seen of the place it would be better to have the operation, if there was going to be one, in a private clinic. I was hopeful that the clinic would be far superior in cleanliness to this hospital. I thought that hopefully we could fix a place for Albina tomorrow at the clinic. The operation would be comparitively small and I was determined to get it arranged before I left India. I would pay for this operation. Nobody else remotely connected with Albina could, so I felt this was the least I could do for her.

Back into the jeep, and shopping in Ranchi. The noise in the streets is deafening, car horns forever blowing and thousands of people about. Ranchi is bulging at the seams with people. Where do they all come from? I've asked myself that question many times, yet amid all this hustle and bustle is the sacred cow, who couldn't care less what goes on around her. While sitting in the jeep in a traffic jam I really studied this sacred of all animals in India. I watched one in particular for about three minutes. Everything it comes across as it strolls around the bustling town it gobbles up. It eats waste paper, cardboard boxes, pieces of wood, rotten vegetables and general garbage which litters the streets. Literally everything it comes across it eats. I'm sure the cow would eat a dead dog if it came across one. Yet so often the sacred cow is a magnificent specimen. Its carcass is perfect. It would fetch the highest price at any cattle market sale in England. They must have more robust insides than us humans. I wonder if they suffer from indigestion. If the Westerner eats food that he feels has even the slightest possibility of being "off" he is soon at his doctor's. No rubbish for him. Here, the cow thrives on it.

While shopping in Ranchi with Sister Bernadette, Sister Michael and Albina, it was my intention to buy Albina a watch. Sister Bernadette had told me that this was her dearest wish. She was aged 24 and had never owned a watch. I intended to put this right. When she tried on one particular wristlet watch I could see she liked it, and I told her it was hers. The look on her face told a story of not quite being able to believe it was hers. I knew she would treasure that watch. In English money it was worth about £6. To Albina that watch was certainly the most expensive item she had ever owned in her life. At the time I told her it was hers she must have felt like a millionairess. This very poor girl from the village of Tongo in rural India just couldn't believe it. At last she was a somebody in India. She had a watch. To see that look on her face alone made it worth it for me to travel thousands of miles to see her. To say she will treasure that watch is probably an understatement. I again felt nine foot tall as I looked at her. If I was her Pappa, as she called me, then the pleasure was all mine. It was now time to get Albina and her friend, who we had left at the Ranchi convent school, to the bus which would take them to Lohardaga. It was back to studies for Albina, but I would see her again, as we would be calling at the Lohardaga college tomorrow afternoon. And then I would be off to Tongo, where I would be spending my last few days in India. But it's been arranged that she will see me off from Ranchi airport when I leave. My abiding memory of Albina as she caught that bus is of her looking at that watch. She just couldn't believe it was hers.

I wanted to do some further shopping in Ranchi. I was now thinking of my family. I intented buying my wife a ring, which I did. I also went to other shops and bought clothes for my two children and grandson. There are real bargains in these shops, but one must barter the shopowners down in price. Never give the asking price for anything in India - prices can be brought down. I'm sure the shop owners expect it, and if it means a sale they will usually drop the price.

Back at the Ranchi convent school I had my usual all-over wash with a bucket of cold water and went to supper. These Ursuline sisters here are so helpful and friendly. Wherever I am in these convents in Bihar I feel among friends. Such devotion to their cause has to be seen to be believed. When I walk past nuns in an English city in future I shall understand more of their lives. I shall, in fact, want to stop and talk to them. After passing the evening in conversation with the sisters it was back to my bedroom to write up my daily diary. I have nearly finished and - blow me down - electricity is cut. In darkness I struggle to find the oil lamp and matches. It's 8.30 in the evening, so it's another early night. How does this state of Bihar survive, I continue to ask myself as I lie in bed. Well, it struggles along under great difficulties - strikes, strikes and more strikes. And Ranchi hospital is in my thoughts again. Was it really that filthy? Well, it was. I've seen it - and seeing is believing.

Day Fifteen   22.11.91

Dr Who and a Scary Journey

I've had the best night's sleep since I've been in India. I slept for over nine hours. I needed it. All at once my back is better. This is how it often is - in great pain for about a week and then suddenly it disappears. So this morning I feel in great shape. After breakfast it's off by jeep to see a doctor in his private clinic. With the X-ray of Albina's arm with me I hoped I had all the necessary information to judge whether it could be operated on. Sister Bernadette and Sister Michael were with me, Albina, of course, having returned to Lohardaga the previous day.

If I expected this clinic to be any cleaner in appearance than Ranchi hospital, then I was in for a big disappointment on my arrival. By Western standards this place was filthy, certainly no different from the hospital. While we were waiting outside the clinic, the general look of the place was very down-trodden. Dogs were roaming about and often coming very close to where we were sitting. These dogs, these most pathetic and so very badly treated of all Indian animals, were forever scratching themselves. Parts of their coats had been scratched away. They were so thin. One was told never to touch a dog, which of course was good advice. Nobody seems to own these Indian dogs and they roam anywhere they please. In this open-air waiting room they were only yards from where we sat. Again I thought of the disease these animals might carry with them. Rabies was always in my thoughts. But I have had great sympathy for these dogs wherever I have seen them on my travels. Nobody cares for them - they are often kicked by anyone who comes across them. No wonder I saw lots of dead dogs in gutters and pavements all over India - these poor animals just give up and die, all skin and bones. I think of my dog at home. She's the lucky one. Here, dogs must be only too pleased to die and be out of it all.

The dirty walls again had to be seen to be believed. Once white, they now looked dirty - more black than white, I'd say. There was dust on the chairs we sat on. I thought once again of my doctor friend at home. I also looked at the two sisters who were with me. They would not know any different. They were both Indians and would accept what they saw as everyday conditions. To a person like myself from England, there was no comparison with British hospitals and clinics. But I continue to be amazed, surprises continue to happen. India has surprises for me most days. To see this clinic in its filthy condition was a complete surprise. And again I hadn't seen the wards.

We eventually got the call to see the doctor. Even inside his office, it looked as though a bomb had hit the place, papers strewn about everywhere. Sister Bernadette and Sister Michael were with me. On showing him the X-ray he wanted to know where the girl was. We explained that she had had to return to her college in Lohardaga the day before. He hadn't looked particularly pleased to see me as I walked into his office. Now he was disgruntled and got aggressive, saying how could he possibly operate on a patient he'd never seen. I accepted what he said, of course. I tried to explain to him that as we had the X-ray with us we hoped he could tell just by looking at it. He then flew into a rage, losing his cool. We weren't in that office more than three minutes. I gradually started losing my temper as well. Who did this man think he was, I thought. The sisters were quiet and accepted him for what he was. Here again I was seeing that people with authority abuse the power it gives them. On calming down after what was a heated argument between us, an appointment was made to see Albina the day before I flew off from Ranchi. Who did this man think he was, I again thought. But I was in his country and I had to accept India for what it was.

I got out of the doctor's office and got halfway to the jeep when Sister Michael came running after me, saying that the doctor wanted 100 Rupees. I coughed up. It was expensive for three minutes, I thought. I thought the doctor's whole attitude had been deplorable. His rudeness and superiority made me think again of the caste system here. He would be of the higher caste. Charging me the fee he did, he was undoubtedly one of the better-off in this country. I could well afford it, but the poor people of India could no way afford that sort of money. The poor are terribly exploited in India. This doctor had no doubt made himself rich from the poor. I was again on the side of the poor in this country. The rich get richer and the poor get poorer. This was the caste system in practice again. Who was this doctor who was so unco-operative? I shall call him Dr Who, as I had no idea what his name was.

On climbing into the jeep Sister Bernadette informs me that it's time to get the jeep insured.

"Is the jeep insurance up for renewal?" I ask.

"Well, as you know, we only managed to get the jeep one week before you arrived and we just haven't had time to get it insured," she says. Had I really been travelling all those miles in a jeep without insurance? This, of course, was another surprise. I'm sure India sleeps half the time. It wants a good shake, but as I've said before I should never be surprised by anything here.

When we arrived at the motor insurance office I asked Sister Bernadette if I could come with her just to sit and listen. Working, as I did, for an insurance company in England, it would be of particular interest to me. I listened alright, but learned nothing, the whole conversation being in Hindi. Here again the attitude and manner of the clerk left a lot to be desired. He was aggressive and rude, just like Dr Who. Why is it, I continually ask myself, that people with authority abuse it with rudeness. I must add that I've only found this rudeness in Ranchi. Shopkeepers can be just the same. I left that office again feeling for the underdog, who in this case was my friend Sister Bernadette. Next door to this insurance office is a garage from where the jeep was bought just three weeks ago. Sister Bernadette saw the foreman of this garage about a noise under the bonnet. Could he look at it, she asked him.

"The whole labour force is on strike. Come back when we are working normally," he told her, this again being spoken in Hindi. On Sister Bernadette telling me this I shook my head. What next, I thought.

The premium of 2,500 Rupees was considerably less than motor insurance would cost in England. At least we had the jeep insured. All motor insurance here is done with the National Insurance Co. Ltd. The thought of driving with no insurance in England makes one shudder. I felt somehow safer on climbing into that jeep again.

After quite a busy morning, I again managed to squeeze in some shopping, buying more presents for home and sweets for the children of Tongo - 1300 boiled sweets. Indian children love sweets. I wanted to give these children something in return for the many happy hours I'd spent with them - one sweet for each child. At the sweetshop, the same rudeness from the owner, unfortunately. He didn't seem to care whether he served us or not. In fact I felt that he actually didn't want to serve us at all. Sister Bernadette and Sister Michael, dressed of course in their nuns' clothing, did not break down any barriers in Ranchi. Why, and I continue to ask myself this, is there this deplorable attitude? I have not found this rudeness anywhere else in India. In fact, in Calcutta people were so hospitable and friendly that they particularly went out of their way to help me. I can't understand it. On talking to the sisters about this rudeness they shake their heads and accept it. To me, though, being a Westerner, it stood out and I can't help wondering why it exists.

Sitting down for lunch at the Ranchi convent school, the meal I was served with was chicken and chips. This was more like it. I actually had a second helping. Time was getting on, so we made our departure for Lohardaga. Sister Bernadette had business to attend to in Ranchi, so she would make her own way back to Tongo in about two days time. It was past 3 o'clock by the time we got going in the jeep. It would easily take an hour for three of us - Sebastian, Sister Michael and myself - to drive through the streets of Ranchi before hitting the countryside, so it wasn't until well after 4 o'clock that Sebastian was able to put his foot down. And even then, we probably reached no more than 20mph.

Those potholes in the roads will slow any driver down. We certainly wouldn't make Lohardaga in daylight.

On approaching one of the villages on the route, we noticed an unusual number of people about, crowds lining the streets as if we were in a built-up area again. But this was a village. We sensed something was wrong. Eventually we came to a halt. We were now stationary and unable to move. The crowds were getting thicker. There was great excitement. Sister Michael then decided to find out what was happening. She soon disappeared through the crowds of people. Police seemed to be everywhere. After three minutes she came back hurriedly and told Sebastian and myself there had been a murder.

"Things are getting worse every day on this road," she said, "murders are becoming quite common. Evidently a gang was on the loose and they had done the killing. "Bihar," stated Sister Michael, will not be safe anywhere soon."

Sebastian then managed with great difficulty to reverse the jeep and go back about two miles down the road we had travelled on. He knew a route that would bypass the village. This road, though, was really a country lane and was probably very rarely used by motor vehicles. By the time we had bypassed the village it was nearly dark. Some of the locals down these country lanes looked very startled on seeing a white face in a jeep. I'll swear they had never seen a white face before. Just before darkness finally fell, and it was getting dark very quickly, I began to think of this gang, who by all accounts had got a clean getaway from the murder scene. Would we come across them, I suddenly thought. We were miles off the beaten track. It began to be a bit unnerving. We wouldn't stand a chance if we ran into them. I was now getting quite worried. If that gang had got clean away from the village, they were somewhere for sure. They could well be out here, I thought. I knew from reading about these gangs that appalling attrocities had been committed, beheading their victims being a particularly favourite way of killing. The sooner we got off this road, the better, and indeed it was with great relief that we finally made it. We were on the main road to Lohardaga again. It was a scary journey, bypassing that village. We could breathe more easily again.

We still had another 20 miles to go and we were forever coming across groups of police, so we assumed the killers were still in the area. Finally we made it to Lohardaga. The journey of 30 miles had taken about five hours and we arrived at 8 o'clock. We were welcomed very warmly by the sisters at the training school. I was given hot soup and bananas. The soup was good - I needed warming up. The night was cool and the whole atmosphere of the journey had been chilly to say the least. I really was pleased to be here. The intention, if we had arrived from Ranchi in reasonable time, was to carry on to Tongo. But it was decided that we should stay the night. The principal, Sister Angeline, insisted on it. I for one was not going to argue with her. It was now nearly 9 o'clock, too late to see Albina, who would be in bed by now.

I'm writing my notes under the oil lamp in my bedroom. What another day it's been. Every day incidents seem to happen. To be alone in a jeep with only two companions on the dark roads of Bihar is something I shan't forget. Meeting Dr Who was also an experience. I now realise I've lost all touch with the world from whence I came. I've now been in India for 15 days. There are no newspapers here, no TV. I think of my wife. How is she? I hope she's not worrying too much about me. But knowing her, though, she will be. I wish I could tell her I'm OK, but there's no way to. One thing I'm really pleased about is my back - all pain gone.   I just hope I'll be alright for my last few days in India.

Day Sixteen   23.11.91

I Return Home With Delhi Belly

All of a sudden this morning at the breakfast table I developed stomach pains. I was doubled up in pain - Delhi Belly had struck. I had to get to the toilet quickly and just made it. I had diarrhoea. I suppose if one spends three weeks in India like I have one can consider oneself extremely lucky if one's health holds up. Apart from my back, which is fine now, thank goodness, I have been in good health. My main worry when I arrived in India was going ill. Illness can completely ruin a holiday, but generally speaking my health had been good. Now Diarrhoea had struck. "Oh God," I thought, "not this." My remaining days in India would be in ruins. I quickly took some pills that my doctor had given me. In fact, I had a good supply of different pills in case of illness. I came well prepared. My doctor had told me I would get diarrhoea. "You're bound to, going to India," he said. I could only take the pills and hope they would work quickly.

Albina had been given an hour off to be with me, as we hoped to leave Lohardaga by 10 o'clock for the journey to Tongo by jeep. It was good to see her again. I thought how pretty she looked. We were now beginning to communicate much better and I could now understand her. We went for a walk in the college gardens. I then told her how proud I was of her. She was determined to pass through this college and achieving that goal was the greatest challenge of her life. She had ambition alright, and when I thought of the background she had come from my admiration for her grew stronger. We had struck up a good friendship over those ten years of writing to each other. Even in the early letters her desire was one day to be a school teacher. She was not too far away from achieving this burning ambition she had. She knew that this was what I wanted more than anything for her. Then, having passed her exams, she would be able to earn herself a reasonable living. This, then, is what she so badly wanted to achieve. If ambition and the will to succeed were her strong points, which they unquestionably were, she would do it. And when she does pass those exams, nobody will be prouder of her than me.

We got away for ten o'clock, Albina and about half a dozen sisters waving us goodbye. The next time I would see Albina would, of course, be the day before I flew off from Ranchi, and hopefully to see Dr Who. I did so want a decision on her arm. I was still very hopeful of a simple operation which would make her elbow as good as new.

On the way to Tongo we were to call at the Gumla convent school. Gumla is a town of about 30,000 people. It is halfway between Lohardaga and Tongo. We had to pick up some papers for Sister Bernadette. All at once, as the jeep was approaching Gumla, my stomach ache struck again. We were now in a built-up area.

"Get me to the toilet quickly," I blurted out. I was doubled up in pain and in the crouched position. I was in a terrible situation. Sister Michael could see my predicament.

"Drive faster, he might not make it. Hurry, hurry," she shouted to Sebastian our driver. I'd got the dreaded Delhi Belly. Sebastian somehow managed to get to the convent in Gumla in record time. As the jeep sped into the convent two sisters were waiting to greet us with beaming smiles of welcome. I dashed in through the front of the building where they were standing. They had their hands together in the usual Indian greeting.

"No formalities," I begged, "toilet please." On hearing of my unfortunate predicament they howled with laughter. The wicked sense of humour of these Ursuline sisters was showing up again. Are nuns like this in England, I asked myself. Surely they wouldn't see the funny side of something as serious as a poor fellow desperate to get to the toilet.

"Through there," they laughed. Sister Michael followed me in great haste.

I was frightened to death I wasn't going to make it. Make it I did, though. I sat on the toilet and howled with laughter. How funny it must have looked. There was I with my trousers half down just making it to the toilet, being followed by dear Sister Michael. As I came out of that toilet I said to Sister Michael, with a wink, "that was a bit close." She replied: "Too close for comfort, Brian. Are you alright now?" I assured her I was. I then joined the two sisters who I'd dashed past in the forecourt and apologised for my actions. They smiled, Sister Michael smiled and I certainly smiled. How funny it all must have looked.

Over a cup of tea and biscuits a white Belgian sister joined us at the table. She, along with the white sister I'd met at Lohardaga, was one of the very few white sisters now in Bihar. She spoke perfect English. She had worked as an Ursuline sister in this convent school for 42 years. She had first come to Bihar in 1935, the year I was born. One cannot try to imagine the good work this very gracious elderly sister has done since coming here. Most of the school buildings were put up during those 42 years. She was so very proud of her achievements. She was the headmistress of the senior school. She told me there were more than 1,500 school children here. She was nearing retirement age, though, and like the other white sister in Lohardaga she wasn't sure whether to go home to Belgium or stay in India. I think she will stay in India. This, she tells me, is home.

"So many changes in Belgium," she says, "I don't like the changes."

Before we left the convent school, this white Belgian sister found out about my stomach ache predicament. She too had seen the funny side of it.

"Take this," she said. It was a small capsule. "You won't have trouble again." She then smiled. "That pill will stop anything," she assured me. On climbing back into the jeep I was struck again by the brick buildings. I really did think before I came to India that the school buildings would be nothing other than mud huts. I had been pleasantly surprised and again I thought how happy the children looked as they played in the playground. I again thought of this white sister. She had given her life to this convent school. Her achievements were here to see. These brides of Christ continue to have my admiration. There's one thing for sure. If these Ursuline sisters do not make it to heaven there is certainly no hope for the rest of us in this world.

We made our way to the local bank in Gumla for me to change some travellers cheques. If one is prepared to live cheaply in India - I'm thinking of the cheaper hotels etc - one could spend many weeks here and not spend a lot of money. It really is a cheap country to live in. Inside the bank, although it was quite shabby-looking by Western standards, everyone seemed extremely efficient and pleasant. We called in at the odd shop, just to see if I could buy anything. Same thing, smiling faces and people generally being helpful. Everywhere I've been in India people have been most courteous and kind, Ranchi being the exception. Don't ask me why, I couldn't begin to answer.

Gumla is not a clean town (is there such a thing as a clean Indian town?), the usual filth and garbage lying about. There seemed to be more goats roaming the streets than is usual in Indian towns. The sacred cow is here - India wouldn't be the same without it. Also to be seen are those poor dogs, plus cats and chickens. What disease there must be in these streets. Until India gets its act together and stops these animals roaming about I'm afraid disease will never be far away.

Back into the jeep for the last part of the journey to Tongo. The scenery really is supremely beautiful and so very colourful. On nearing the convent school I had the feeling of coming home. On climbing out of the jeep the sisters came to greet me. It was handshakes all round. Sister Sushila then took my suitcase - I can't lift a thing here. She took it to my bedroom and there, neatly folded, were my shirts, trousers and socks etc, which she had washed for me. Sparkling new, they looked. Since I've been in Bihar I've been extremely well received at the other convents and made so very welcome. But to me this Tongo convent school was special. I was happy to be back here again amongst so many friends. I really did have the feeling that I had come home.

I lay on my bed this afternoon and dropped off to sleep, which is most unlike me. I was woken by Sister Michael. I feel like calling her Auntie. She had brought a bucket of water for me to have a wash down. What I would give for a hot bath. I know I keep saying that, but I feel so very dirty at times. When I get home I'll just soak up a hot bath and realise what I've missed. At the supper table there is much laughter amongst us all. With Sister Bernadette away at Ranchi there are now 15 sisters.

"You will soon forget us when you get home," says Sister Vianney.

"I never will," I say. "How could I possibly forget someone who to get my attention deliberately spills hot soup over me." They all laugh. Sister Albina looks straight into my eyes and says "Don't forget us, will you Brian." At this particular time - would you credit it - Sister Vianney nearly spills soup over me again. There is so much happiness here. These brides of Christ are forever laughing. If there is real happines in this world - and I know there is - then these Ursuline sisters have found it.

As we leave the supper table Sister Sushila says: "Come Brian, let's play some cards."

"Gambling, eh?" I say.

"Only a bit of fun," says Sister Michael. I can't play cards - never could. I try my best, though, and get hammered. The way the sisters shuffle these cards - well, it couldn't have been done better in some London nightclub. It's 8.30 and I say goodnight.

"Don't forget the special church service tomorrow morning," says Sister Angela. I couldn't say no, I didn't want to say no.

"Goodnight, then," I say. I'm in bed for lights out at 9pm. I'm finishing my diary under my oil lamp. The Divine Sisters of Tongo are in my thoughts again. Sister Albina had said 'please don't forget us'. There's never any fear I'll ever forget them. Good friends in life are sometimes not easily found. Well, I've found a group of extra-special friends. I would go through a brick wall for any of them. That's how much I think of them.

Day Seventeen   24.11.91

Sunday Celebrations

Up at 6.15am for a wash and breakfast at 7am. Today is a Sunday, but a different Sunday from usual. Normally, there are three morning Mass services on a Sunday, but today there are only two. There was the usual 6.30 service which the sisters attend every morning, and today there was a 8.30 service which I was told was a celebration to God. It seemed to me very much like an English-type Harvest Festival service, where prayers and thanks are given to God for feeding us from the land we live off. Only here in the Indian countryside living off the land has an extra significance when the land is the peasant farmer's small plot. As I have said before, if they didn't feed off their land they would starve.

We all gathered outside the village Catholic church and there were hundreds of people there. All had come from the surrounding countryside and many had walked miles. This celebration to God was one of the highlights of these poor people's year. We were to form a procession going into Tongo's countryside. The walk took about half an hour. The Tongo convent girls school and the boys school were out in force. There was singing and laughter as the procession made its way out of the village. The local priest and two curates seemed to be organising the event, the sisters for once not involved in what was going on.

What a colourful crowd of people there was in that procession, the women all in their bright saris. All the colours under the sun were being worn by them. The children also looked particularly clean in their Sunday best clothes. Indian women love their saris. It was noticeable that some wore jewellery as well - jewellery is very special to Indian women. I'm not saying that it was expensive jewellery they wore, because I knew they just couldn't afford that. But they did wear it, including beaded necklaces and bangles. I also know that in order to own jewellery they would work for years just to be able to buy a ring or necklace. Their justification for owning jewellery is that if they got into a desperate situation where there was no food coming off the land, at least they could go to the village market and try to sell this jewellery they had worked so very hard for. This way they could earn some Rupees to help them through the desperately hard times that do come from time to time.

When the procession finally started there must have been nearly 1,000 people going to this church service. I still can't get over the fact that just about everyone in Tongo village and the surrounding countryside goes to church. They would have to be ill to miss a service. Also, Sunday is the day of rest and nobody works here on that day. The way these families work in the fields, they deserve their Sunday off.

Down this country lane the procession walked and then, there on a slight hill was an altar built of stone and draped with flags and ribbons of many colours. Set in the colourful countryside, this altar looked a picture. These features, combined with the saris the women were wearing, made it seem as though everything was in Technicolour. All these colours seemed to blend in perfectly. This large crowd of people then gathered round the altar. There were seats, of course, but not nearly enough. Hundreds of people were left standing. I then settled down to the longest Communion service I've ever been to. It took nearly four hours. I was then told by Sister Angela, who was sitting next to me, that the priest had welcomed me at the start of the service and hoped I was enjoying my stay in Tongo. I was the only white person on that hill attending the service - all those chocolate-looking faces. Amongst all that colouring I must have stood out, but I knew I was in such a happy environment that it didn't matter what colour I was.

Sitting through a service of nearly four hours can be a fidgety experience for me. To sit there and not understand what's going on can be trying to say the least. Sister Angela had told me that the service would in the local language of Oron. She then informed me that she and many of the other sisters didn't understand Oron either. I then consoled myself by thinking that if the Ursuline sisters didn't understand what was going on, what chance had I got? It made me feel slightly better knowing that my ignorance of the local language was shared by others.

After about two hours there was a break in the service. During this break, who should pounce on me but Albina's brother's five-year-old son Ambrose. He was at the service with his grandmother, Albina's mother, and other members of the family. When Albina's mother saw me I was immediately smothered by her warm embraces. She is such a small woman that I must seem a giant to her. She just wouldn't let go of my hand. Sister Angela told me later that she said how lucky Albina was to have met me. I then told Sister Angela that I was the lucky one for having met Albina and her family. I then realised more than ever that if there was any luck going round I'd got it, being born in England as I was, and certainly not these poor peasant people.

Since I've been here in the Indian countryside I've noticed that the only people I seem continually to come across are those from the lower castes. There are certainly none of the Brahmins, the very highest caste, which forms six per cent of the Hindu population in all India. These people really do have the top jobs in the country, often in government and industry, and they are also extremely rich. The other upper castes, which amount to 15 per cent of the population, are also considered to be at the top end of the social scale. Often they are landowners, merchants and shopkeepers. These castes have a reputation for harsh exploitation of the lower castes, who really have been wickedly exploited. No doubts about it, unscrupulous landlords have crucified the lower castes by charging them excessively high rents, so that the poor people in the countryside can barely scrape a living off the land. Where are these upper castes in the Indian countryside, I've been asking myself. In truth, they are just not here in this part of Bihar. The lower castes seem to be left well alone in this Tongo area.

When one is born into the caste system in India there is no escape. Albina's parents are part of the 52 per cent of the population in the lower castes in this country. In the cities these lower castes could be employed as labourers or servants - not, in all honesty, meaningful jobs. These people know their status in life and seem reasonably contented with the knowledge that they will never break out of the system. All the lower castes in rural India are peasant farmers, but I'm told the situation is changing, never more so than for the Dalits, otherwise known as the Untouchables, who make up 18 per cent of the population. Their status is so low that for them to work they must take demeaning jobs like human excerment disposal, burning the dead, sweeping and cleaning, and picking the dead - human and animal - up off the streets. Gandhi tried his hardest to rid the country of these poorest of the poor, re-naming them "Harijans", "children of God". But change is slowly on the way. The humiliations suffered by the previous generations of untouchables are now not being accepted by present and future generations, who in the state of Andhra Pradesh will not tolerate this injustice any longer. But in other areas on India change is slow. In some villages the Untouchables are outcasts. Nobody will tolerate them or speak to them and they are shunned even to the point where the lower castes cross the road in order not to have to talk to them.

So what's the difference, I ask myself, between the Indian caste system, with its shades of discrimination, and the Apartheid system until recently still practised in South Africa. In South Africa one was judged by the colour of one's skin, the white man prospered and basically lived off the black man. Apartheid was putting people into certain groups depending on the colour of their skin. In God's eyes we are all equal - not so in Apartheid, and not so in the Indian caste system. If Apartheid was evil, then the caste system is, too. I would perhaps prefer to call it unfair and unkind. The Untouchables and lower castes are treated unfairly and exploited by the rich upper castes, and are forever unkindly kept in their place, never to escape the system. By an accident of birth one can be an Untouchable and live a life of sheer misery. If in God's eyes we are surely equal, Apartheid and this caste system have a lot to answer for. If change in the caste system of India is on the way I can only hope it's peaceful change and not a bloody revolution.

The service finally over, I walked back to the convent school with Sister Angela. I say goodbye to Albina's mother, who I know in all probability I will not see again. Tears flood her eyes. She was proud of Albina alright. Her daughter was trying to break away from the poverty she was born into, hopefully to stand on her own feet and earn her own living. Albina's mother and father must have made great sacrifices in allowing their daughter to stay at school nearly until the age of 20 and then go on to college. So often children work on the land with their parents when their school days are over. Not so Albina. She was fortunate to get to college. It must have been decided by Albina's parents that their daughter's education was more important than marriage. My admiration for Albina's parents on hearing of their sacrifices for their daughter is immense. They are giving her the chance of escape, and hopefully she will make it.

During the walk back to the convent Sister Angela asks me if I'd care to go for a walk with her this afternoon, so we fix a time of four o'clock. Now Sister Angela is a most attractive-looking woman so I was most interested in why she chose to devote her life to God. Why is it that the elegant Sister Angela should turn her back on the life she was born into in order to dedicate herself to the Lord. I looked forward to my conversation with her with considerable interest.

After lunch I'm in my bedroom looking out of the window and I see the compound wall, this, of course, being the brick wall that stretches all the way round the convent school. As Sister Bernadette had shown me previously , the wall had been damaged by vandals - undesirables, she calls them. From my window, the damage looked considerable. Anyone could walk into the school grounds and take anything they wanted. If violence comes to this area of Bihar as it has to the north of the state, then the sisters here will need protection. In Lohardaga the college not only has a massive brick wall all the way round it, but guards to protect the college at night. Here, the Tongo convent is very exposed. How can I help to raise £3,000, which is the figure required to repair this wall and extend it up to eight feet high? Nothing would give me greater pleasure than to raise money for the repairs to this wall when I get home. I could do a sponsored walk, like I have done in the past for local charities. But I had to face the reality that although people have been so very generous to my sponsored walks in the past, I do not think I would get a very good response for a walk to raise money for a convent wall in India.

This afternoon I keep looking repeatedly at this broken wall from my bedroom window. If only I could repay these Ursuline sisters for their wonderful hospitality towards me. Then, all at once, it comes to me that Sister Bernadette has deliberately put me in this bedroom for me to gaze out of the window and look out onto the broken wall. Well, if she was being crafty it was having its effect. I would have to think up a way of raising money for that wall. Doing a walk was not the answer. I had to think up something else, but what, I kept asking myself. Hopefully I shall find the answer.

At four o'clock I'm waiting for Sister Angela in the school playground and she doesn't show up. I've been stood up by a nun, I thought. There's always a first time for everything. Sister Michael and Sister Teresa, who is staying at Tongo for a few days, ask me to go for a walk with them. Sister Michael then reminds me that my stay here will soon be up.

"Do keep in touch, won't you," she says. The short walk into this beautiful countryside only takes about an hour. The sun is out, the weather is perfect. I cast my mind back to England right now. I think of cold, wet and foggy days. I'm sure when I get home I will close my eyes and think of southern Bihar. What peace there is here - I'm away from the madding crowd. I'm forever being told to bring my wife next time. What a pity she hasn't been able to share with me the experiences I've had on My Indian Journey. I must keep writing everything down about the day's happenings on my holiday of a lifetime.

This evening I say at the supper table to Sister Angela: "Where were you, then?" She didn't seem to know what I was talking about. Then, all at once, she remembers. " I couldn't have been very important to you," I say. At this point Sister Vianney was in the process of serving my soup. She howled with laughter that I'd been stood up, and I so very nearly finished up with hot soup all over me again.

All the sisters can now see the funny side of my being let down by Sister Angela and soup nearly being poured over me again. Sister Angela is very apologetic about letting me down.

"Another time," she says.

"You would only forget again," I say. All this is said in good harmless fun and jest. Nobody takes offence here. Any mishap I have continues to make the sisters laugh. Sister Michael (Auntie) winks at me as if to say 'you came for a walk with me, didn't you Brian'.

After a quick game of cards where I again get mercilessly thrashed by the professionals It's off to my bedroom, followed by Sister Sushila. She inquired whether I needed any washing done before I left. I now only have two days left in Tongo. Sister Sushila tells me that she is going to write to me when I get home. I don't think I could ever possibly forget Sister Sushila. She has been absolutely marvellous to me. I'm sure that whenever my back goes again I shall be thinking of her, her soft hands doing wonders for me. The same applies to Sister Vianney. Whenever I see soup being served up I shall think of her. I have a special memory of each and every one of these sisters. Here on the sub-continent My Indian Journey is coming to an end - two more days here and I leave this idyllic spot I have found in deepest India, and I love it here. As I climb into bed just before lights go out at 9pm I'm finishing my daily diary. Right now I think of this convent which will be forever in my thoughts. I think of that compound wall. How can I help, I keep asking myself. How can I raise money to make this convent secure with repairs to the wall? I shall think of something - but what? That is the question.

Day Eighteen 25.11.91

The Old Priest and a Silly Walk

This morning at the breakfast table I have a good look at all the sisters and think to myself 'have I really been living in convents for nearly two weeks?' They are tucking into their rice with their fingers, as usual, and forever twirling it round in the bowl before they eat it. I couldn't eat rice their way, but they really do love their rice. Every meal seems to be rice for them - they just cannot get enough of it. Also, I've noticed what appetites these Ursuline sisters have - no dieting for them, and no fears of putting on weight. Eat up and be merry seems to be their attitude. In no way do they seem to be concerned about their looks - no vanity here - although some of them are quite attractive.

At about 8 o'clock most mornings I can hear the sisters at prayer in the chapel. Also to be heard at this time from the classrooms is the singing of the schoolchildren. I've learnt since I've been here that Indian children love to sing and music seems to be very much in the blood. With their singing flowing through the convent and blending with the sisters' open prayer, I'm reminded of the film The Sound of Music. The von Trapp family would be perfectly at home here. There's such joy and happiness here that I can almost see Julie Andrews singing and running through the corrridors.

Every day I learn something new. I was under the impression that Sister Bernadette was the one in overall charge here. Admittedly, she is the senior school headmistress, and as she invited me to stay here I naturally assumed she was senior to the others. But I'm told that Sister Albina is the superior for the general running of this convent school. I've had many conversations with Sister Albina while I've been here and at no time has she asserted her authority over the other sisters in my presence. This lovely lady is kindness itself. She is forever asking how I am. Can she do anything for me, she asks, 'please don't be afraid to ask', she says. During many short talks I've had with her I have discussed numerous subjects. Arranged marriages have been talked about at length, as have the caste system, all the religions in India and poverty. I have sat with her on the veranda in front of the main building, where the sisters often pass the time.

Sister Albina has also told me that none of the money the sisters earn is ever seen by them. Sister Sushila had previously also told me of this. Apparently their earnings go automatically into the general running of the Tongo convent, so as I've been with her again this morning I brought the subject up.

"We are so very pleased to give the money we earn to the convent," she says. "I only wish there was more money so we could make the school bigger and better. There is so much work to do here." I agreed with her here, because although the school buildings look in good condition, that is only an opinion formed by someone like me on first seeing this convent school. Beneath the surface, as I've already mentioned, nothing seems to work properly. The plumbing system here is in a terrible state, no toilet works properly and water pipes are forever bursting. Sister Albina is a remarkable lady. Many times I have inquired where she is, only to be told she has gone for a lie down. I gather her heart is not good, but she shrugs off her illness and regains her energies to resume her work, which after all is her life. But I have realised on many occasions while talking to her that she is not well. Of all the sisters here I have found her the most interesting to talk to. She too has mentioned the compound wall. It is falling down in places, she says. Oh God, I thought, how can I find money to help repair that wall. It was now becoming an obsession with me to repair that wall - goodness knows how, though.

After lunch I'm walking in the grounds of the whole school, which includes the Tongo boys school and the village Catholic church, when I come across an elderly white gentleman sitting on the veranda of one of the smaller brick and wood buildings near the boys school. This is also the residence of the parish priest. I immediately get talking to this man. He informs me that he is a retired Belgian priest who came to this area 52 years ago. It surprised me that he was white because I thought I was the only white person here.

"I can't get out much now," he says. "Too old for anything," he laughs. He tells me he will probably die here. "This is my country now," he says. He speaks very good English. In fact, I felt at times as though I was talking to an Englishman. Although he was probably well into his 70s his mind was good. His knowledge of India was considerable. We drift into conversation about Bihar. He informs me that it really is a corrupt state.

"Politicians - don't talk to me about them. They do nothing," he says. The violence in Bihar is dreadful in some areas, he says. "I'm afraid it will come here one day, and what chance will these simple peasants have? They will be no match for these violent thugs who roam and terrorise wherever they go.

"But don't underestimate these simple people here. They might well turn. They would not give up their piece of farmland for anybody - their land is their life. They would not bow to unscrupulous landlords' demands," he says, adding: "If the poor peasant farmer makes 20 Rupees a week, landlords often demand nearly half of that, which leaves the farmer hardly enough to live on.

If he does not pay up he is thrown off his land. This indeed happens in many areas of Bihar, but not in this Tongo area, fortunately."

The priest then goes on to explain that in Bihar gunmen really do kill indiscriminately, with whole villages wiped out. People just disappear. Young girls are being forced into prostitution, appalling atrocities having taken place. Then there are the Naxalburi gangs. The Naxalite uprising started in a suburb of Calcutta with a Communist splinter group. Their targets are often these unscrupulous landlords who have given the peasants such a bad time. If caught, these feudal landlords are often killed in a horrible fashion, undergoing many hours of torture before finally being put out of their misery. Also, some Naxalites have been captured and taken to police stations, never to be seen again. Law and order has broken down in many areas of Bihar. This old priest, though, has a genuine fear of the violence coming to Tongo. I for my part hope this fear is unfounded. What chance would these peaceful country folk have against armed gangs. I think, too, of the sisters and schoolchildren. It makes me shudder. I can only hope that violence never comes to this area and that Tongo remains peaceful forever.

Having read in the newspapers while in Calcutta of the continuing violence in Bihar, the priest was only confirming what I already knew. As he talked about the villages, one of them sprung to mind - Bhagalpur, where there were riots during the 1989 General Election that killed more than 2,000 people. Bhagalpur is in north Bihar. Although it is really a town, Mafia-type gangs controlled the polling booths. People were told how to vote and were unable to argue. I had read of these tragic events well before I left England. In one village 100 children had been rounded up and never seen again. Politics and thuggery go hand in hand in Bihar. What happened to those children nobody knows. But this compound wall in Tongo now has extra singnificance. I must somehow get that wall completed, if only to give the sisters and children some protection against armed gangs if and when trouble does come to this area.

I left the retired Belgian priest in mid-afternoon. What an interesting conversation that was. I feel like a good walk. I've done so little walking since I came to Bihar. I did manage to do quite a lot in Calcutta. I happen to believe that walking is the finest exercise any of us can have. At home I walk miles and love it. Sometimes before I start work in the mornings I'll walk ten miles or more - and when I'm in training for a marathon walk it could be 15 miles a day. I do these walks three times a week, although in the weeks leading up to a marathon I could be out walking every morning. My doctor friend once told me that people just didn't do enough walking. There's no need to jog or play squash, he said, just have a good walk, a brisk walk. I took his advice five years ago now and I believe I'm as fit as anybody my age.

The sisters had warned me about walking too far. The Tongo convent school is on a main road, although one wouldn't call it that in England - it would be thought of more as a country lane. Go two miles either way, I was advised. So, it's on with my walking boots. I turn left at the main gates and I'm away. The reason for this warning is that stray animals come down from the forests and have been known to attack people. The animals are tigers, bears and wild pigs. The children who walk to school go in groups. These animals will not attack children in groups, I was told, only a person seen out walking on his own. I was also told not to stray too far from the convent school. I was, after all, white and although I couldn't imagine any of these peasant people having a go at me, one could never be sure. I was, after all, still very much in a strange country, with strange habits and different cultures. I mustn't tempt providence. I must keep within the safe boundaries as I've been told.

Now my walk. The way I walk is not a country stroll - it is a road race-style walk. I learnt to walk this way while briefly a member of Leicester Road Race Walking Club. This type of walking is great for exercise. I'm not saying I wiggle my backside the way road race walkers do. Road race walking is an Olympic sport. These walkers can walk faster than some people can run. But when I'm flat out I can get near to it.

On starting my walk at the main gates I'm into the countryside in no time. The time is about 4 o'clock, the heat of the day is disappearing and I'm really motoring. It feels good - I'm really stretching myself, of course. At this time of day the Tongo school girls are going home in their large groups. I don't think they have ever seen a walk like it. As I'm approaching them with my quick walk they all start to giggle. On meeting an Indian person one is obliged to greet them with the most courteous of Hindu gestures, the Pranam, placing one's hands together in front of the face and saying Namaste, which means 'greetings'. Well, every 100 yards or so, whenever I saw a group of schoolgirls approaching I would place my hands in front of my face and say Namaste. Well, you can imagine how funny it looked - me walking my fast walk, which these schoolgirls had undoubtedly never seen in their lives, and giving them greetings. Of course, once I was past the girls, the giggles turned to uncontrollable laughter, their laughter rolling round the countryside of Tongo, hundreds of Tongo schoolchildren laughing at me.

I must have been a peculiar sight. I had a great rapport with these girls, with their happy, smiling faces. All barriers have now broken down during my stay here with them. 'What an eccentric fellow this

Englishman is', I'm sure they thought. Well, if I can make them laugh, why not? It was alright by me. I must also have looked a very strange figure as I walked up and down the road outside the convent and into Tongo village. The locals just stood open-mouthed. Some waved, some stared in disbelief. One of the locals, his English being quite reasonable, actually asked me what I was doing. When I explained that I did this kind of walk for the sheer enjoyment of it he shook his head, muttered something and gabbled in Indian. To people in the Third World it must have seemed very strange to see somebody from the Western world walking in a silly way for the sheer enjoyment of it all and making a complete fool of himself. But the pleasure was all mine. I just love walking and back at the convent school I felt much better for it.

After my usual wash down with one of Sister Sushila's warm buckets of water it was time for supper again with the Divine Sisters of Tongo. At the supper table Sister Alphonsa and Sister Vianney told of the funeral they attended today of a white sister from Belgium who had died recently. This sister had done wonderful work in the community where she lived. She had lived at a convent school about 50 miles from here. She had been buried in the village to which she had given virtually her whole life. Apparently she had lived in India for nearly 50 years.

"I don't think I've ever seen so many people at a funeral," said Sister Alphonsa, "nearly everyone was in tears. She will be missed in that village." Once again I think what extra special women these sisters from Belgium must be to devote their entire lives to God. To have left their no doubt comfortable, middle class homes in Belgium, these white Ursuline sisters had to be devoted to their cause. I had met two white Belgian sisters while I'd been in Bihar - I had nothing but admiration for them.

The ages of the sisters at this Tongo convent school range between 30 and 58 years. When I arrived here nearly two weeks ago the younger sisters were perhaps shy and withdrawn. I don't think they knew what to make of me. They are now full of confidence in talking to me in English, laughter never being too far away. After supper I play cards again, or try to, I should say. These sisters are so good at this game. They tease me, go round me in circles and come in for the quick kill at the finish. No money is played for, of course, because they haven't any. I say goodnight and I'm in bed by 9pm. Tomorrow is my last day here, and I can't believe it.

Day Nineteen 26.11.91

Last day in Tongo

My last day in Tongo - how the time has flown by since I've been here. Well, there's a saying that if one enjoys oneself the time goes quickly. The days spent in these convent schools have been one of the most wonderful experiences of my life. I've enjoyed my time stay here, there's no doubt about that. I must admit I did have slight reservations about staying at a convent. Those fears quickly receded, though. I couldn't have been better received and looked after anywhere. There is a sadness within me that this is my last day here. I shall never forget the Ursuline convent school, Tongo, as long as I live.

This morning I had the task of giving the Tongo school children the 1,300 sweets I had bought at Ranchi. Every one of these children was to receive a sweet. In the absence of Sister Bernadette, who was still away in Ranchi, Sister Vianney, the assistant head school teacher of the senior school, had all the senior school out of their classrooms and into the playground. She made a speech informing the schoolchildren that I would be leaving tomorrow and that I was to give each and every one of them a sweet. This immediately brought smiles to their faces. Indian Children love sweets. Sister Vianney's speech was being translated for me by Sister Sushila. She told the children of my fear of flying and said the whole school would pray for my safe return to England. Please come again, she said, as we have all enjoyed your visit so much. In my reply I told them that if I ever came to India again I would bring a suitcase full of sweets. When translated, this of course made the children excitable and happy. Speeches finished, every one of the pupils came up to me on the platform to receive a sweet. This was indeed a luxury to them. It's very doubtful that their parents would have enough money left over from the meagre earnings from their little plot of land to buy any sweets. When all of them had received a sweet there were about 50 sweets left. I threw them into the air, and the scramble for them was chaotic. The kids screamed with laughter and the look on the faces of the lucky ones was as if gold had been discovered. To see those excitable children getting those sweets was worth travelling all these miles to India to see. They then sang a song, a farewell song. Believe me when I say it was a very moving experience.

The very same procedure happened at the junior school. One had to see the 600 smiling schoolgirl faces to experience the moment fully. These kids are so happy here. I notice again how spotlessly clean they are, considering that they walk miles from the countryside to get here and come from the poorest homes imaginable. But they love this convent school. I don't think there can be a school anywhere where children are so happy. I've certainly never come across it before in my experience of schools. Sister Scholastica, the junior school headmistress, then made a speech saying much the same as Sister Vianney. The children then also sang a farewell song. Once again their singing voices float around the beautiful Bihar countryside. Seeing these Indian schoolchildren and also the happiness here has been very much part of my holiday. The Ursuline sisters must take the credit for what happens here.

Walking around the school grounds I'm foever bumping into the children. They greet me with the customary hands clasped in front of the face, saying

Namaste. One can never walk round this convent with hands in pockets because this greeting happens hundreds of times a day. I always have to have my hands ready for it.

Many times while I've been here I've popped into the classrooms at the invitation of the sisters. I have often been bombarded with questions, usually about England, and these children are always interested in the Royal family, who I've found are generally regarded with great respect in India. I've also been asked many times about my home and family in England. I hope I have always been able to answer their questions. They all seemed reasonably happy with my replies.

The Ursuline sisters, as I have explained previously, originated from Belgium, having arrived in India in 1903 - just four of them - the Ranchi convent school being the first to open. Then, with expansion, 24 convent schools were opened in Bihar. It was about 50 years ago that a convent school was first opened in Tongo, this being a girls senior school. Years later a junior school opened. Of the 1300 children at this school, 250 of them are boarders who come from country areas so far away that it would be impossible for them to walk here.

The boarders' day is not unlike that of the students at the Lohardaga training college where Albina is. They rise at 6am, draw water from the well for washing and of course attend prayers. Even before school starts at 9 o'clock there is two hours of study. There are usually four lessons in the morning, followed after lunch by three further lessons. During the evening there is gardening to be done. Pupils have their own little patch of garden to look after. They are supposed to get free time after supper, which is at 6pm. Free time can often mean more studying. By 8.30 they are in bed with lights out. It's a hard life being a boarder at Tongo. Ask any of them if they'd change it, though, and they would definitely say no. Yes, being at this school, even with all the manual work the pupils have to do, can be enjoyable. These children prove that. They love being here. They wouldn't want it any other way.

When the children reach the age of 16 their lives are often already laid out for them. Many leave school and marry. These marriages are arranged by the parents, as mentioned previously. But just before they leave school, they take an exam which is equivalent to an O' level or GCSE. So it can either be marriage or further education, based on the result of an exam. Some of the lucky ones, on passing the exam, may get secretarial work and have to move away from their homes. This would also apply to those who wished to become nurses. After all, Tongo, being rural India and miles away from any big town, has nothing to offer these children. Tongo consists of a shop and a few wooded mud huts and that's it. Some of the children might even train to be a schoolteacher like Albina, she being the lucky one, having managed to live and study at Lohardaga Ursuline Training College. The nearest college, at Chainpur, which these children would automatically have attended, is closed by industrial troubles. But only about ten per cent manage to find work when they leave school. The other 90 per cent usually marry.

The sisters here tell me that the education the children receive is certainly not wasted. Even if they cannot obtain work they are often able to help their parents and family members with advice which only a good education can bring. The children's parents, having never received any education whatsoever, may well be illiterate for their whole lives. Also, the one who goes to school from any particular home may be just one of six children in a family who gets an education. This may, of course, create jealousies in some families because one child is able to go to school and another one isn't. This situation is far from perfect, but it is better than nothing. Just one child being educated can make an enormous difference to a family's home, with many children passing on the knowledge they have learnt from school and in some instances teaching their parents to read and write. Today, my last day here, has been quiet. I've been walking the school grounds for the last time. The Ursuline convent school here in Tongo is the centre of all activity in the village. The village has no facilities at all. Everyone comes into the school grounds for whatever service they may require. The small hospital, called the dispensary, is run by Sister Fredric. It has a dozen beds. I walked into the dispensary this morning. Sister Fredric took me to see her patients in their beds. Three schoolgirls were there with malaria, along with a village peasant farmer. Sister Fredric was not sure how to treat this man. He was shaking violently, with hot and cold sweats. If he did not improve, a doctor would have to be sent for from Gumla. Sister Fredric does wonderful work in her dispensary, looking after not only the schoolgirls but all the villagers for miles around.

I walk by the big Catholic church for the last time. My memory of the church is the sheer number of people it can hold. On Sundays it is packed. Why is it that a church in India, and this goes for all churches in India, can be so full of people when in England the opposite applies? I do not know the answer. But what I do know is that for these farming community people going to church is a very important part of their lives. Maybe, being so poor, they feel more of a need to pray. I do know their lives are very much controlled by the weather. As I've said previously, without the rains and sunshine at the appropriate time nothing would grow on their little plots of land.

Strange what one thinks about when one is alone in a foreign country. Of course my family are constantly in my thoughts. Many years ago, though, during my army National Service time in Hong Kong, the highlight of the week was knowing how one's home town football club was getting on. If that club won its weekend game it was as though all was well in the world. Peterborough United (Posh) are now in the Third Division of the Football League. I've always followed their results with great interest. It's strange, though, how one associates oneself with one's own football team when abroad. All those years ago in the Far East it was very important for me to know how Posh had got on. When one is abroad this is important. I have these feelings of years ago now, but there's no telling how the Posh are faring, there being no newspapers, TV or radio of course. My son will no doubt bring me up to date when I arrive home.

Also in my thoughts as I walk round the school for the last time is what a shame it is that Action Aid pulled out of this part of India three years ago. Sister Bernadette asked me only a few days ago if I could entice them back. The sponsorship by charities like Action Aid was wonderful for us, she had told me. Apparently nearly a third of the children here in Tongo were sponsorhip children at one time. I remember those three years ago because Action Aid had asked if I would sponsor another child, as Albina Kujur was no longer part of the sponsorship programme. Action Aid moved to southern India and this is where my sponsored child is. I was slightly disappointed, though, as I would have preferred to sponsor another child in the Tongo area. I was told at the time Action Aid pulled out that a French charity was taking over all the Ursuline convent schools in Bihar. Sister Bernadette knew nothing about this. Action Aid did such good work here, she told me.

When Action Aid was involved with the sponsorship of these Ursuline convents of Bihar, that little monthly sum of money paid by sponsors towards an education for the children of this area was very important towards the running costs of the convent schools. About 50 per cent of all sponsorship money was spent on food for the children, with two full meals of rice a day, which would also include vegetables from the school garden. Part of the sponsorship money also went on school uniforms, books, games and medical expenses. Now there is no sponsorship money and to me this is very sad. The schools in this area do get some help from the Indian government, but not nearly enough, and I believe some financial help comes from Belgium. These convent schools can do with more financial help. Sponsorship works, I've seen it. Through sponsorship Indian children are getting an education. Albina Kujur is a classic example of what sponsorship of a child can achieve. She was lucky to join a sponsorship programme and now she is on the verge of earning her own living.

"please ask them to come back," Sister Bernadette had asked me, "we need them." I look again at these convent school buildings and I see decay. Money to help repairs here is urgently needed. Sponsorship supplied just that.

Later on this afternoon I went for a quick walk, one mile one way outside the convent and one mile the other way - yes, my silly walk again. I just had to walk into the beautiful Tongo countryside one last time. In the distance the peasant farmer is at work in the fields with his wife. The fields are full of these people working the land. I know the farmer has an extremely hard life in the country areas of India, but in many respects his wife works even harder. Her life can be sheer drudgery. She works the fields, she runs her home, she cooks for and looks after her family - her day is never finished. Indian women are put upon. Often the real heavy work is left to a woman, whereas in the Western world a husband will help his wife in this respect. I well remember when I was met at Ranchi airport. Albina virtually insisted on carrying my suitcase to the jeep waiting outside in the car park. For one so small as her my suitcase was heavy. I had to insist that it was my responsibility to carry it and not hers. I really had to prise it from her. To Albina it was a natural thing that she should carry my suitcase, however heavy it was.

Just before supper I packed my suitcase. It was a struggle to get everything in. I didn't realise I'd bought so many presents. I virtually had to sit on it to close it. Into my bedroom comes Sister Sushila with yet another bucket of warm water. What a friend this sister has been to me, she being the one who has done all my washing, rubbed oils on my back and struggled up the stairway at least twice a day with buckets of water for me to wash myself down with. Nothing is too much trouble for her. She really has been a bit special to me. It's probably a little unfair of me to single out particular sisters, but I must also mention Sister Bernadette, Sister Albina and Sister Michael. These four have seen to my every whim. I know some of the sisters here have not even had a mention in my diary, but that doesn't mean I think any less of them. Since I've been here I've had the feeling of belonging to one big happy family. It's difficult to explain my feelings, but I shall remember the happiness I've found with these 16 sisters forever. These Brides of Christ, themselves often born into appalling poverty, are devoted to their cause. I've been in the near-secret world of their lives for nearly two weeks and, as I've said before, it really does remind me of the film The Sound of Music. In this convent school it doesn't matter what time of the day it is, a classroom somewhere is singing. These Indian children just love to sing. The Ursuline sisters here have brought and incredibly happy atmosphere to this convent. I've seen it, believe me.

This evening was the night of the Last Supper. I looked at the notice board and in large letters it read: "God will take care of you dear Mr Brian. Have a safe journey. A happy arrival home." The sisters had made a special cake for me. I sit down with these 15 Tongo sisters, Sister Bernadette still absent. Sister Vianney pours out my soup. I keep my fingers crossed that I won't get it all over me. Every time she pours out my soup I'm a nervous wreck. Trouble is, she doesn't concentrate on what she's doing. But I shall miss her, just like I will the others. After my soup, toast and bananas I cut the special cake the sisters have made and they all clap their hands. After what I jokingly called the Last Supper, I now had a surprise for each one of the sisters. When I was with Sister Bernadette and Sister Michael shopping in Ranchi I asked them what present I could buy for them to remember me by.

"They only want the simple things in life. Your love is everything to them," Sister Bernadette had said. But I badly wanted to buy something for them, so it was agreed I should buy them each a jar of face cream. On presenting them with their jar of cream after supper I knew instantly I'd done the right thing. Their delight on receiving those jars was not unlike a child receiving a present. They were ecstatic with shrieks of delight.

I was told to remain seated at the table and the 15 sisters gathered round and sung me a farewell song. This was an incredible experience for me. I just looked at each and every one of them as their beautiful voices sung this very moving song. The emotion was now building up inside me. After the song each sister came up to me and kissed me on each cheek and then on the lips. I tried to make my farewell speech in a clear voice, but my voice was faltering. I had a lump in my throat. I was choked with emotion and words just wouldn't come. If ever I wanted a clear voice to thank them for their marvellous hospitality it was now. But I was emotionally struck by their sincerity. These were my friends, the best friends any man could have. I'd never met anybody like them. Tears were in my eyes. I managed to stammer out a few words of thanks, said goodnight and retired to my bedroom.

I am now in the process of completing my diary for my last evening in Tongo. Lights will be out in a minute. I think again of the Divine Sisters of Tongo. There's one thing I do know - these Ursuline sisters did not need face cream to make them beautiful. These sisters are the beautiful people of this world. If there were only more people like them in the world today, the world would be a much better place.

Day Twenty   27.11.91

Goodbyes

Up earlier than usual this morning for 5.30am, Sister Sushila knocking on my door with the usual bucket of warm water. The sisters had asked me the previous evening if I would like to go to the 6am Mass with them in the chapel. I had told them I would be pleased to do so. Part of the service was in English, which I understood had been done for my benefit. The parish priest of Tongo took the service, my name being mentioned in prayer for a safe journey home to England. I certainly wasn't looking forward to all those flying hours again, but I'd had a safe flight from England, so I could only hope that my flight home would be equally so.

After breakfast the superior, Sister Albina, made a final speech asking that when (not if) I came again, would I bring my wife Kathleen with me. I again stammered out a big thank-you to everyone at that breakfast table. The emotion was building up in me again. Then as a final gesture the sisters again took turns to kiss me for the last time. At this point I particularly thanked Sister Albina for the wonderful time spent with the sisters and the way I'd been so very well looked after. "please don't forget us," she said, "remember you will always be in our prayers. We will pray for you that you arrive safely home." What beautiful words from a lovely lady, I thought. My suitcase packed, Sebastian took it from me to put in the jeep. Outside in the playground it was as though nearly a quarter of the school was there to see me off. A final wave and we were off, with Sister Sushila and Sister Michael also on board. It was nice having them with me.

Also in the jeep was Sister Angela, who was to be dropped off at the Gumla convent school. As we had left the convent at 8.15am we saw many of the children walking to school from the country areas and waving furiously at me - they all seemed to realise I was on my way home to England. As the jeep pulled away from Tongo village I wondered whether I would ever visit again. I would dearly love to, of course, but only time will tell.

After saying goodbye to Sister Angela at Gumla we were on the road to Lohardaga. The roads hadn't improved any, but now my back was fine. Sister Michael told me that two sisters from another convent school in this area were seriously injured and in hospital when a jeep in which they were passengers hurtled off the road and into a ditch. This had happened only two days ago. I wasn't surprised - anything could happen on these roads. There can't be worse roads in all India than those in the state of Bihar. These roads are particularly dangerous, especially when going over bridges. One slip by Sebastian and I'm sure we would have been over the edge. There really were large holes in most of the bridges we crossed. If one travels anywhere by road in Bihar they are certainly taking a chance with their lives.

On arrival at Lohardaga Ursuline Training College to pick up Albina, who we were taking to see Doctor Who about her arm, we had tea and biscuits with the principal and several sisters. I had got to know these sisters on previous visits. I thanked the principal for all she was doing for Albina and she promised me she would make sure Albina was eating properly. She repeated that Albina was very frail.

"I will keep a special eye on her for you," she said. At this point Albina joined us and we were ready to go. I said goodbye to all the sisters and we began the two-hour journey to Ranchi convent school.

Ranchi, as I've said before, is a small town but simply bulging with people, thousands of them everywhere. Again I thought to myself that until India sorts out this massive over-population problem it will always remain a Third World country. I thought also of the children growing up in these towns and cities of India. What chance have they got, I often asked myself. Very few children in India get any education at all. They grow up to be illiterate and scrounge a living from the streets, usually by begging. Contraception must be the answer to India's problem. As long as thousands of babies are born in India every day there can never be an answer for this over-populated country. China allows just one child per family in its attempt to beat the continuing problem. Maybe India should do the same.

On arriving at the Ranchi convent school we had lunch and made our way by jeep through the continued hustle and bustle of Ranchi's traffic for the appointment with Dr Who. With Albina were Sister Sushila, Sister Michael and myself. At last, I thought, something positive could be done for Albina's arm. I went to see this doctor full of hope. After a long wait in the open-air waiting room the four of us were finally admitted to his office. Again, his attitude was quite deplorable. He looked at the X-ray and then, very clumsily, I thought, examined Albina's arm. He wanted to know how high she could lift it. He pulled at Albina's arm and she winced. He could see that Albina couldn't lift her arm above waist height. The doctor then infuriated me by saying that the arm wasn't a liability and then said: "What do you expect. She's only a village girl. Lots of village people have worse things happen to them than that. This statement really got my back up. I could sense the caste system rearing its ugly head again. Albina came from a village and was in the lower caste of Indian society. This Dr Who was part of the upper caste. What infuriated me most was that he thought he was superior to Albina, which he undoubtedly was, but only in terms of his profession. Being a doctor in India demands respect, but he didn't have to be so blatantly rude about it. Because of the shades of discrimination he abused his position and I was angry.

I looked the doctor straight in the eye and said: "It's because Albina is a village girl that I want to help her. Whatever the operation costs I will pay for it. This girl means an awful lot to me and I want peace of mind by knowing that everything that can be done has been done. Tomorrow I leave for England. I've come to you for your professional advice. Can the arm be operated on or not?" By now I was losing my cool. All I wanted was his advice about what I thought was a comparatively simple operation. He could see that his attitude had upset me and immediately changed from being aggressive to being a doctor full of sympathy for his patient. This was better. I had called his bluff and we were now on the same wavelength. I had stood up to this doctor. We could now talk sensibly. Again he took Albina's arm, this time more caringly. He asked her to see how high she could lift it. He then said that in his opinion it was better that the arm was not operated on. He told me that the elbow would not necessarily go back into its socket. He then explained that because of the long delay - it was nearly three years since the accident - he could not guarantee the success of an operation. In all probability Albina would be in pain - far more than she was in now. Rightly or wrongly I thought that a comparatively simple operation would make her arm better. I realised that the doctor was the expert and that I had to take his advice. I reluctantly agreed that the elbow was best left alone.

We all trooped out of the doctor's office. I'm sure we all felt disappointed that nothing could be done for Albina's arm. Hopefully, she had many years left in this world. Her arm would be a liability for the rest of her life. Not being able to lift anything, or even comb her own hair or play netball, which they play at the college, was restricting her from leading a normal life. I thanked the doctor. By now I had cooled down. He had changed completely himself once I had stood up to his arrogant attitude. As we were climbing back into the jeep he actually smiled at me as he walked past us. I had once again seen the unfairness of the caste system. By my standing up to him I had won his attention and respect. If Albina had gone into that clinic on her own, goodness knows how he would have spoken to her. The caste system puts people into different groups and social classes. I'll never come to terms with the unfairness of it. I'd seen the caste system at work again today and it saddened me.

Late this afternoon I went for a walk with Albina through the Ranchi convent school grounds. In the short time I've been in India I have begun to understand her better. She tells me that her ambition is to come to England one day. I know, though, that she will never be able to afford to come herself. I told her to work hard and concentrate on her studies for the next two years. There was no need for me to have said that because, as I've said, her determination to become a school teacher is so intense that the thought of failing has not entered her head. It's quite remarkable, knowing her background, that she could possibly be a schoolteacher. What an achievement it will be for her. The country must have progressed if a poor girl from deepest India can qualify to be a schoolteacher. I know how hard she's worked. Marriage, at present, is not for her - maybe one day. But nothing will stand in the way of her achieving the ultimate ambition in her life. Having met her, I know she can do it. I realised once again that this was a girl to be proud of. I suppose one can say that Indian children sponsored by a charity like Action Aid are the lucky ones. Let me assure the reader that while there are perhaps admittedly some children more fortunate than others, which will always happen in a sponsorship programme, I consider it was not Albina's luck to have me as her sponsor, but my great luck to have found her.

My supper was served in my room tonight. There is a meeting of sisters from all over Bihar tonight in the main hall. Dear Sister Michael (she will always be Auntie to me) appears with the food tray - chicken and chips. Not bad, eh, I thought. This was indeed another Last Supper, my last supper in Bihar. While I'm eating, Albina appears with a friend. I knew I'd seen this girl friend of hers before. She was from Albina's village and she was in Tongo that day Albina's family gave me that wonderful welcome. Her friend has been studying at the Ranchi convent school for nine years. From what Albina told me, her friend hopes to be a sister herself one day. At this point Sister Bernadette appears. She apologises that she couldn't be with Albina and me today and explains that she has had much work to do in Ranchi. It's nearly a week since I saw Sister Bernadette, so we had some catching up to do. But she will be able to take me to Ranchi airport and see me off tomorrow.

My last evening in Bihar ran true to form - the lights go out and I'm groping about for another source illumination. My guests say goodnight. Tomorrow I start my return journey to England. I shall soon be re-united with my family. I shall have such a lot to tell them. As for Albina, it's going to really hurt when I say goodbye. I'm proud of that girl, I really am.

Day Twenty-one   28.11.91

Till We Meet Again

I am writing having just boarded an Indian aircraft at Ranchi airport bound for New Delhi. It should have left Ranchi at 1.30pm. I've just had a four-and-a-half hour wait. The 'plane finally took off at 5.50pm. Everything, of course, is late in India. I should know by now. In fact, I should be used to it by now. I am writing up my diary with the 'plane having just taken off. I'm not exactly comfortable sitting in a 'plane again. I know I never shall be comfortable, but I do believe the fear of flying has receded a little. Perhaps, with all the air travel I have done recently, one can get used to it. Anyway, I'll put the flight out of my mind and concentrate on the day's events leading up to it.

Last night, in bed under my mosquito net, I just couldn't get to sleep. There must have been a hole in the net. Mosquitos have a real buzz about them, particularly at 3 o'clock in the morning. They were buzzing inside my net all night. I got up to re-make my bed a couple of times. Mosquito really is an appropriate name for them, with their victims - in this case me - easy prey. They really do have a Spitfire buzz about them and in the middle of the night that noise is very real indeed.

After breakfast at the Ranchi convent school I took Albina and her friend shopping in the town. I wanted to buy something for my daughter Julie and my grandson. I hadn't got a clue what to get them, though. I hope I've bought them something useful. Clothes are usually the most appropriate present to buy, so this is what I did. I also bought Albina a very bright yellow spotted sari. She being very small, a few adjustments would have to be made. These alterations can be made by her in the embroidery classroom at college in Lohardaga. She would certainly look good in it, only I would never see her wearing it, of course. We then walked back to the convent school, once again sometimes being pushed along by the sheer mass of people. Yes, Ranchi is a busy place. Seeing all these people here, I wonder, though, whether it is because they literally have nowhere to go. They are certainly not shopping. They wouldn't have money for that. Even crossing the road can be hazardous. I'll never forget the hustle and bustle of Indian towns and cities, but in a strange way I shall miss it.

On dropping Albina's friend off at the convent school I asked Albina to take me to the cathedral, which is right opposite. Inside, it was a magnificent building. Albina knelt down and was in prayer for several minutes. I sat in the pews and thought of home and the many hours of flying time ahead of me. Aboard the 'plane I'm now in God's hands again. That cathedral was certainly the appropriate place if I wanted to pray myself. I tried to console myself with the thought that if there was a 'plane crash, at least I'd seen India and met Albina. On the outward flight I hadn't even had that fact to comfort me. I've had friends die early in life and suffer great pain while dying of cancer in their beds. Perhaps being aboard an aircraft crashing into a mountain is the quickest way to go, but dying as an old man in my bed is more appealing. Would I make it back to England? Only time will tell.

We walk round the cathedral looking at old Biblical pictures on the walls. Albina then tells me it's time to go. It's time for me to get ready for my journey home. Ranchi airport calls and my time here is coming to a close. We have an early lunch - my flight to New Delhi is at 1.30pm, so it's best to get to the airport in good time. Lunch, chicken and chips, was cooked especially for me.

I really did appreciate that meal, my very last meal in Bihar. I seem to be forever saying goodbye at present. After more handshakes with the Ursuline sisters at Ranchi convent school we are off through the streets and the usual squalor of Ranchi for the last time.

Travelling with me to the airport are Albina, Sister Bernadette, Sister Michael, Sister Sushila and Sister Fredric, who had made her way by bus this morning from Tongo. I was going to get a good send-off. I take a last look at India in daylight because by the time I get to New Delhi later today it will be dark. On the short trip to the airport I see the usual rickshaws, buses, lorries, stray dogs and the sacred cow. There is now a sadness within me. All these thousands of people I see before me will soon be gone forever, and I shall miss it, yes, all of it. India will, I know, be very much a part of my future life. My 22 fabulous days in this country are coming to an end and some of the best friends I've made here are to see me off from the airport.

We arrive there just after midday and wait for the 1.30pm flight. I take Albina for a cup of tea. Sister Michael then says that Albina wishes she was coming with me.

"She wishes she was coming to England with you, Brian," she said. I looked at Albina. There was a look of sadness alright. We were then told by the airport officials that the Ranchi to New Delhi flight was running two-and-a-half hours late. This immediately put Sister Bernadette in an awkward position. These four sisters, along with Albina, dearly wanted to see me off from the airport, but it would mean them hanging around for another two-and-a-half hours, and even then it could be longer - nothing goes on time in India. I also realised that the sisters had a long journey back to Tongo, and they would have to drop Albina off at Lohardaga first. Personally I didn't think it safe for the sisters to be alone in a jeep at night in the Bihar countryside. I had travelled on these dark roads at night and it could be a scary experience. I therefore insisted they leave and get on with their journey. Sister Bernadette argued that it was okay for them to wait a little longer, but I knew it would be very unfair to let them stay. I again insisted and we walked to the jeep to say our goodbyes.

At the jeep Sister Bernadette shook hands and kissed me and got in. I had a lot to thank her for - it was because of her invitation that I was able to come to India. Sister Fredric did likewise. Sister Michael, the affectionate "auntie", hugged me and said "have a safe journey home". Next was Sister Sushila - more kisses. Whenever my my back plays up I shall think of her.

"Goodbye, Brian, and God bless," she said. Last, but not least, Albina. This was probably the unhappiest moment of my entire stay in India, a quick hug and kiss and she said "Goodbye Papa and love to Kathleen and your family". She actually said that - she was learning her English quickly. I told her I would write to her as soon as I arrived home safely. She understood and nodded. She climbed into the jeep and I shut the rear door. By now I was feeling quite choked. I shook hands with my friend Sebastian, there were a few shouted goodbyes and they were off, till we meet again, I thought. I followed the white jeep until it was just a speck on the horizon and lost in the Ranchi traffic. I waved furiously until they were no more.

I walked back into the airport building. What a shame the 'plane was late. Albina had only ever been to an airport once before and that was when she met me at this very place. I'm sure it would have been more exciting for her to have seen me board the 'plane and watch it take off, away into the skies. It was not to be, but I felt happier that they had gone when they did. They would at least be able to do part of the journey to Tongo in daylight. Once back in the airport I had the feeling of being alone again. It was a peculiar feeling. I had been alone for most of my early time in India and it hadn't bothered me. I couldn't understand it - perhaps it was brought on by saying goodbye to a group of special people who I'd grown so very fond of. Would I ever see them again, I asked myself. One thing was for sure. Having come over 5,000 miles to India to see Albina I wasn't ever likely to lose contact with her again. We would communicate through letter writing and hopefully we would one day meet again.

Just before the sisters left the airport building Sister Bernadette had spoken to an Indian businessman. She had asked him to keep an eye on me if he was going to New Delhi. So, during a long afternoon of hanging around an airport I was not entirely alone. This businessman and his wife were a very charming couple. He worked in the steel industry. He gave me his card and I knew I'd found another friend. These travelling businessmen have been kindness itself during my travels in India. This couple certainly helped me pass the time. Eventually the 'plane came along from Calcutta. All aboard, the aircraft took off at 5.50pm, four-and-a-half hours after its scheduled time. The 'plane seemed packed with briefcase-carrying businessmen, probably going home for the weekend.

I'm continuing my writing with the 'plane having touched down in Patna, in north Bihar. A lot of the businessmen get off to be replaced by more businessmen, again all carrying briefcases. On the 'plane I bought an English-language newspaper. This being the first paper I'd read for nearly two weeks, I had a lot of catching up to do. I'm now writing in New Delhi airport. The flight from Patna took one hour, thirty-five minutes and was perfect in every way.

I was a little worried at Ranchi airport to read on posters that there was to be an air strike on November 29. All Indian flights were to be grounded for this one day. I was assured, though, by my Indian friend that my British Airways flight would not be affected. This was a relief, because with my flight touching down at New Delhi at 8.45pm I now had another four-hour wait for my flight from New Delhi to Gatwick. This would take the day of departure to November 29, the day of the strike. I now wanted to get home as quickly as possible and hanging around in New Delhi for an extra day did not appeal to me. But I need not have worried.

On arriving at New Delhi I thanked the businessman and his wife for looking after me. On collecting my suitcase I pushed through a very crowded airport. A guide from the travel company was due to meet me here, and there he was shouting "Mr Holdich". It was the familiar face of Kev, the man who first picked me up at this very airport when I first landed in India three weeks ago. He told me that we had to get to the other side of this huge international airport, so we made our way to his car with my luggage. This little car ride took about 20 minutes. He then checked me in for Gatwick, the flight being at 1.55am. With an hour or so to spare we went for a cup of tea in the airport restaurant. Kev wanted to talk about cricket, and I was quite happy to oblige. India had beaten South Africa twice in the three-match series. He was happy, but said South Africa would be a force to be reckoned with in a year or two's time.

Kev then told me he would like to come to England. He was very determined, he said - would I meet him at Gatwick and could he stay with me in England? I must add here that Kev's travel company had been superb in meeting me wherever I'd been in India, so thinking this was the least I could do, I agreed to his wish. The time was now drawing near for the last part of My Indian

Journey, to England and home. I shook hands with Kev, thanked his company for being first-class and waited for my flight, a flight of nine hours. I was getting nervous again, pressure building up once more. I wanted this last flight out of the way - let's get it over with, I thought. England beckoned, my time in India was up. England was my home, and I was ready to come home.

Day Twenty-two   29.11.91

New Delhi To Market Deeping

Well, true to form, nothing in India is ever on time, catching aircraft being no exception. The 'plane bound for Gatwick took off from New Delhi at 3am. I really was leaving India on the last stage of My Indian Journey. Market Deeping was drawing nearer. All that hanging about at Ranchi I could have done without. I think just lazing around airports is a terrible waste of time, and I've had my share of it in the past few hours. Two flights in less than 12 hours is going some for me. I'm now writing my notes on the flight home. I must do something. This is why I'm writing right now - I'm too tense to sleep. I look around the aircraft. We have been flying for about an hour. Just about everyone is snoring their heads off. Why can't I be like these people, I ask myself. Why can't I relax more? After all, if the 'plane does crash into a mountain it doesn't really matter if one is asleep or not, does it. It's probably better if one is asleep - at least one wouldn't know anything. Having said that, I don't think one would know much even if one was wide awake, either.

At Delhi airport I got talking to a retired Indian businessman who lives part of the year in London and the other part in New Delhi, where he was born. He is with his wife, having spent three months in India. Here again I've found it a great comfort to be in an airport talking to people who are probably just as nervous as me about catching a 'plane. And, of course, it does pass the time. This man must have done extremely well in business. Spending one's retired life in two countries must be expensive living. India is home, he says, and always will be. But his children grew up in England and he's lived in London more than 30 years. He keeps in touch with his roots, he says. I look for him on this aircraft and he, like everyone else, is fast asleep.

As I sit here on this 'plane my mind can't help wandering back over my three weeks spent in India. So much has happened in such a short space of time. I took my son-in-law's camera with me to record on film what I saw. I just hope I got it right - what disappointment I shall have if nothing comes out. I look through my diary pages of those days, reminding me of what actually happened. I have memories that will last a lifetime. Did I really meet Mother Teresa? That really was a stroke of luck, even if I did nearly get myself killed in that cemetery, or so I thought. That man who so casually got talking to me in Calcutta and with whom I thought I was in great danger for those few seconds did, in fact, take me to Mother Teresa's. So perhaps I should be thanking him. At least through being drawn into conversation with him I was to meet someone who I'd read about and admired for years. How many people from my part of England, Lincolnshire, have been in conversation with this great lady? There can't be many, if any. I felt spellbound in her presence. If someone had asked me five months ago to name the five people in this world I would most like to meet, Mother Teresa would have been one of them. I shall never forget the way she greeted me. I have met a supreme human being and I have seen the work she does for the dying destitute in Calcutta. She is a very frail old lady, who I know does not enjoy the best of health, but hopefully this great Christian will live many years yet.

Once the aircraft had taken off from New Delhi the captain explained that the flight would be taking a different route home to Gatwick. He mentioned that one of the countries we would be flying over would be Iraq.

With the flight now two hours old, we could be flying over that country right now. The Gulf War is still in everybody's mind, the liberation of Kuwait having come only a few months ago. At this particular moment I'm thinking of Sister Angeline, the principal of Lohardaga training college. She had told me that Saddam Hussein was not evil, but that what he had done was an evil act. I think of the people of Kuwait. What must their feelings have been when Saddam's troops marched into the country and started killing, looting, raping and pillaging. Surely this was evil at its worst. I admired Sister Angeline so much for being so sincere in her beliefs and honesty and I know that ascribing evil to fellow human beings is against Christian teachings, but - and I know this is a preposterous thought - imagine if Saddam Hussein had invaded England; Would the English not think he was evil. What I do know, and history tells us this, is that evil has to be crushed. England would not be the free country it is today if it had not fought evil. Tyranny has to be beaten. My own fear is that world has not heard the last of Saddam Hussein. It was interesting to read the thoughts of many of the leaders of the Church of England⁻ during the re-taking by Allied troops of Kuwait. They had said this was justified. My thoughts are that evil has to be stood up to. If not, the consequences could be horrific.

While all around me are asleep, I think of Ranchi hospital. I had to see it to believe it - such filth I'd seen there. How can patients be treated and cured in conditions such as exist there. That poor pathetic dog, with its body sores, was scratching itself and limping through those corridors. How unhygienic it all was. Thinking of Ranchi Hospital, I automatically think of Dr Who. I never did know his real name. I took Albina to see him about her arm. I shall never forget his words: "What do you expect. She's only a village girl. Lots of village people have worse things happen to them than that," he had said. His remarks had stirred something within me. For the first and only time in India I was angry. This poor defenceless girl who I'd brought to see him was of the lower castes of this country. People of the higher castes will probably always talk down to her, but not while I was with her they wouldn't. Dr Who had abused his privileged position. To my way of thinking a patient is a patient irrespective of caste. But the country was India and I had to respect its ways.

All sorts of happenings are flashing through my mind as I think back over those three weeks. I can't sleep on this 'plane, but I'm really desperately tired. Hopefully if I keep writing I might possibly drop off. I think of Calcutta - what a city, so infectious. Mixing with its millions on those crowded streets I was alone, yet not alone. Amidst all its squalor and misery I found a basically happy people. How could they laugh with so many undernourished people just roaming the streets. I was forever speaking to people who just seemed pleased to be talking to me. This Black Town, as it was known, it's beautiful women and children, who were just beggars on the streets surviving somehow, I'll never forget them. What on earth had they got to be so happy about. Winston Churchill, on writing to his mother, had said that having seen Calcutta once, he would find it unnecessary ever to see it again. Two centuries ago Robert Clive, soldier and governor of west Bengal, called it the most wicked place in the universe. As for me, I couldn't get enough of it. I really would love to visit again some time, malnutrition and all.

I'm still very tired and I haven't dropped off yet. Must keep writing. Into my thoughts come the Ursuline sisters of Bihar, not just those at Tongo but all of them. Giving the children of India an education and serving God, that is their life, and at no time was religion thrust on me while I stayed with them. The happiness I found in those convents and the sisters' wicked sense of humour took me completely by surprise. If I expected nuns to be as serious as the impression one forms of them in England, I was certainly in for a surprise. These sisters were the happiest women it has ever been my pleasure to be with. The Tongo sisters are my friends for life. I feel honoured to have met them.

I think of the Taj Mahal in all its splendour. Is there a finer building in the world? If there is, then I've yet to see it. A man built it in memory of his wife. Well, his wife must have been a beautiful lady because the Taj Mahal is a monument of staggering beauty and seeing it was breathtaking. I think of Amin, my guide. There really could have been a most unpleasant incident right in front of that magnificent building, two men in heated exchanges and neither giving way. Fortunately it didn't quite get out of hand, but Amin was right when he told me the Taj Mahal must be protected at all times. It must be India's major tourist attraction. We live in a world where terrorists can strike at any time. India would never be quite the same without the Taj Mahal. I'm still seething, though, when I think of my stupidity in taking a photograph of the 'plane at Dum Dum Airport, causing the security guard to confiscate the film. I had seen the Taj Mahal, but I did not have my own photo of it.

On thinking of Amin, that other superb guide comes to mind - Sunny, what a character he was. He really did want to be Prime Minister of India. He enthralled me so much with his tour of New Delhi. I wish I could see him again for the pittance I gave him when we shook hands to say goodbye. But at that time it was my first day in India and I didn't really understand the currency. I was mean in the extreme, but in all honesty I didn't realise it. Through my ignorance of Indian money I had offended him. I am deeply sorry about that. Too late now, though. The damage has been done.

The aircraft has been in flight nearly nine hours now. It's taken longer coming back to Gatwick than it did when I flew out. People all around me are waking up and getting restless. I envy them their sleep. I've had none and now I feel shattered. Again I think of India, so many memories. What of Albina Kujur? It was because of her that I went to India. Finally meeting her at Ranchi airport was a magic moment in my life. People might ask me when I get home if I was disappointed in her in any way. My answer to that question is no way - in fact, she was an even nicer girl than I'd hoped she would be. My thoughts about her were not ones of disappointment at all, even though we couldn't communicate too well at times. I've flown thousands of miles just to see her. I might possibly never see her again, but there is a closeness between us that will never die. I know that we will stay in contact through writing letters to each other. I'm proud of her for what she's done and what she hopes to achieve. She has lived her life in Mahatma Gandhi's India, the countryside of which he spoke so highly. I think of that extraordinary day when I was welcomed by Albina's family to her humble home. I also think of that colourful landscape of the Tongo area. How beautiful it was.

At least writing my diary on the aircraft has passed the time on a long journey. The time is 11.15am Indian time. By putting back my watch six hours makes it 5.15am British time. The 'plane is nearing Gatwick Airport, another stage of My Indian Journey done. I now feel really tired. What I'd give for some sleep. Over the tannoy the captain tells us he's unable to land - too much traffic, apparently. The way he said it made it sound like one of those supermarket car parks one drives around looking for an empty space that isn't there because the car park is full. So because of the traffic the 'plane keeps circling the airport. The captain eventually gets the all-clear to land, so down we go. Another perfect landing and I thank God because I'm safely home on English soil once more.

I'm continuing my diary in the comfort of Gatwick's lounge. I glance outside and it looks like a typical English November day, damp and uninteresting I would call it. I think of all the sunshine I've just left. Every day, apart from slight rain in the morning at Agra, the weather was hot. Not an unpleasant heat, either. When I arrived here about an hour ago after getting through customs I fully expected to see my wife and son. While all around me were embracing each other I couldn't find her. Where was she, I thought. I couldn't wait to see her. After about half an hour of no Kathleen I decided to telephone home. On picking up the 'phone my wife thinks I'm calling from India. When I tell her I'm at Gatwick she says I'm a day early.

"The travel company said you would be arriving home on November 30. You've arrived a day early," she said. Well, I was dead tired and I couldn't explain. She said she would get Richard, our son, from work and drive to Gatwick immediately. The journey would take about two hours, so I'm sitting here in this lounge. I've tried to sleep here, but I can't. My head is in a whirl. I can't relax, even now. How can I relax when I'm waiting to see my wife. I don't want to miss seeing her as she comes through that door.

A scream rang out through Gatwick lounge when she saw me. Obviously being away from each other undoubtedly makes the heart grow fonder. On the way home it was all questions. My daughter Julie came to see me this afternoon with my grandson - great excitement as the presents were given out. My wife told me that she had only received three cards the whole time I was away. I do know that I wrote home on each of the first seven days I spent in India. Once I got to Bihar and the convents, however, I knew that cards sent from rural India would probably take weeks to get home, so I never bothered. My wife said that if just one card had got through from Tongo she wouldn't have worried so much. I could see the strain I had put her through. My children told me she had worried herself sick while I was away. I again had feelings of guilt, but she knew what going to India meant to me. I think in some of her real black periods while I was away she had wondered whether she would ever see me again. Thinking about that incident in the Calcutta cemetery, she wasn't far wrong either.

My wife had asked me during the afternoon whether I had had a bath lately. I said the last bath I had was in Calcutta two weeks ago. My wife then told me I was stinking the room out.

"You have an awful smell to your body. It's like a stale, musty smell of someone who hasn't washed for months. Please go and have a bath," she had said. Well, all those wash-downs with buckets of water over my body had only partly kept me clean, so this afternoon I've really spoilt myself with the most satisfying bath ever. I'd have given anything for a hot bath in those convents, particularly when I'd hurt my back, just a simple hot water bath. I'd really missed it, one of those everyday things we in England take so very much for granted.

Once out of the bath I went for a lie down on my bed. Surely I would be able to sleep now. I was dreadfully tired. I'd had a hot bath, but I just couldn't sleep. My mind is in turmoil. I can't get India out of my thoughts. On lying on my bed I think that maybe I've had a dream - I was certainly in the appropriate place for one, afterall. All that travelling - more than 11,000 miles to the back of beyond and back, all those different flights, more than 26 hours in the sky, my fear of flying perhaps deminished a little - but I'd come through everything unscathed. In the security of my own bed I realise I am safely home, but I feel jet-lagged, I feel utterly washed out.

This evening - yes, I'm still awake - I've been telling my family of countless experiences. So many questions, so many answers to give. While talking of these experiences I've been eating nuts picked by the sisters of Tongo from the convent garden just before I left. On eating them, I feel that if I closed my eyes I would still be in India. If rice was the sisters' favourite food, then these garden nuts were a close second. After every meal at that long table we would always finish by eating nuts. Yes, those nuts reminded me of India alright. India will, I know, always have a special place in my heart. I feel right now that a part of me will always be there. In the introduction to this book I quoted what the American writer Mark Twain had said of India. He said that India was the one land that all men desire to see, even by a glimpse would not give up that glimpse for all the shows of the rest of the globe combined. Well, I'd seen that glimpse, fleeting glimpses as I travelled through an absolutely fascinating country. On day 22 My Indian Journey is now finished, my glimpses will last forever, far more than any thousands of books could ever possibly tell me. What an experience it has been for me. I feel that I can speak of India with some authority. Mark Twain was unquestionably right - I certainly wouldn't give up my glimpses of India. So intrigued have I been that I want to return.

Reflections

It's now August 1992 and nine months have passed since I arrived home from India. I've had a lot to reflect on. Ever since I arrived home on November 29 last year my thoughts on India have never been far away. I don't think I every quite realised what a mammoth task it is to sit down and write a book. I knew that getting My Indian Journey down on paper would take up a lot of my time. But, having never written a book before, I had little idea just how long it would take. Well, it's now finished - or is it? I'm sure I'll alter something, or perhaps my memory will remind me of something I'd completely forgotten about. That is the trouble. I must have written my story many, many times - perhaps six times in some areas. I never realised the frustration of being a writer, completing perhaps a whole chapter and then, having read and re-read it, having to scrap it. One aims for perfection. If a tiny sentence is not as I feel it should be, I've started again, perhaps going back three or four pages. My manuscript is now ready and being printed. It's been hard but rewarding work. If I hadn't been employed I'm sure I could have completed the book within four months of arriving home, but my work came first. Any spare time has been spent on my book - mornings, evenings, all hours - you name it, I've done it. I think I've been driving my wife mad with the constant talk of India and my book. At times it's dominated all conversation. But I just had to get it all down on paper while it was fresh in my mind. And, of course, I wrote pages and pages of notes each day while I was in India, which I've found invaluable. So what I write now are refections on My Indian Journey nine months on.

Catastrophe - that's how the newspapers describe it. A chilling United Nations report in April warned the world that unless immediate action was taken to control spiralling numbers, the very future of humanity would be at risk. There are just too many people in this world. The growth will happen almost entirely in the Third World, where poverty is rife. Ethiopia, where thousands are starving to death and will continue to starve, has a current population of 49 million. Over the next 30 years the population is expected to rise to 126 million. In the whole area of eastern Africa, the projected increase is expected to be from 197 million to 542 million. The report, by the UN Population Fund, said: "Like a gradient between high and low pressure in the atmosphere, the result could be a rising wind of migration circling towards the north." In other words the industrial countries of Europe and North America had better be prepared because the rush of immigrants to the wealthy industrial nations will become uncontrollable.

Dr Nafis Sadik, the Population Fund executive director, described the prospect as a nightmare and criticised the Roman Catholic church for outlawing contraception. Having been to a Third World country, India, and seen a nation bulging at the seams with vast over-population, I have to agree with Dr Nafis. I have seen the human misery and degradation of a people who live well below the poverty line in cities numbering millions of people. People really do lie down and die. Babies really are born hungry and many die. In India, 70,000 babies are born every day. How many of them are really wanted? Many, as soon as they are old enough, are thrown out onto the streets and into a life of begging. Somalia is the latest African country to provide horrific pictures on our TV screens of little children and babies dying through malnutrition. I'm sure I speak for many of us in our comfortable English homes when I say that seeing those appalling pictures makes one wonder if the world's gone mad. As much as the West helps with vast amounts of money, the population growth of Third World countries will not go away. Those TV pictures have a terrible effect on me. I feel ill, depressed and angry. Surely the answer is contraception. China has shown the way. Surely other countries could follow. I know the Roman Catholic church is against contraception, but I just wonder whether some of its leaders would have second thoughts if they were in Somalia right now.

It's interesting to hear the views of Dr George Carey, the Archbishop of Canterbury. He chose to question the Catholic doctrine on birth control. He has said: "I try to understand the Roman Catholic position. I don't fully understand it. I do believe it is a very important issue they have got to address. No civilised society can really stomach those pictures of dying, emaciated children with any comfort at all. I feel ashamed and grieve inwardly every time I see them, wondering what we can do. We cannot say that population is nothing to do with it. Of course it is. I believe that the issue of population is a challenge facing us all." Dr Carey was due to meet the Pope last April and these issues of over-population were to be discussed. My own thoughts are that over-population and poverty undoubtedly go together in the Third World. Cut down on future population and the poverty will decrease. If something is not done soon the world will really be on a horror course. Millions will die and continue to die. This population crisis threatens us all - let's do something positive now. Family planning must be the answer. The warning signs are there. Children shouldn't be allowed to die in the 20th century through starvation. Surely the world has progressed since time began. On seeing those dreadful pictures of dying children I wonder whether the world has progressed at all.

When I think of poverty in India I think of those cities of millions of people. That very first day, on that tour of New Delhi - I can still visualise the face of that shockingly ill seven-year-old girl who was skin and bones and had a look of sheer terror in her eyes as she saw me sitting in the back seat of that Morris Ambassador. She scratched at that side window with a fear I'd certainly not seen before. Believe me when I say that there are millions and millions of children all over India living a life of sheer misery. What goes through the minds of seven-year-olds when they are abandoned on the streets to beg to survive, just to get through the day? Their lives must be hell on earth. Hell, we are told in the Bible, is for the next world. Well, some of the kids I saw in India are experiencing hell right now. Yet, surprisingly enough, children in India manage to survive. Indian children are the great survivors. Take those children I befriended in Calcutta. I bet anyone right now that I could go to that very same Nehru Road and there they would be, surviving somehow into a life of sleeping rough and begging, to be spat at and despised by not all but some of the more affluent Indians.

On Christmas Day, while eating my leg of turkey, I really did think of those street kids of Calcutta. Would their Christmas Day be different to any other day? What would they be doing right now, I asked myself. My Christmas Day was partly ruined by thinking about those children. They might not even have known it was Christmas. I sit at home often thinking of those two particular ones, that brother and sister I shouted at to stop following me. How cruel I was. On watching my TV set I'm shown pictures of starving children in Somalia and makes me want to switch off and forget. But I can't and it makes me feel guilty, guilty that I have the lifestyle I have. Yes, children in many countries of the world are dying at the rate of thousands a day. Children in the Third World are getting a raw deal. Surely more could be done with the Western world's rich resources. I know the West does help, but it's never enough. Surely, then, family planning must be the answer. Take the children in some South American countries. In some cities in Brazil, where the poverty is just as bad as in India, death squads openly go round killing them to clear their streets of abandoned children. It really doesn't bear thinking about, does it. In Bogata, Columbia, the abandoned children have taken to living in rat-infested sewers. The stench in those hell-holes and the living conditions are too unbearable to contemplate. Apparently the children come up from the sewers at night to raid dustbins for food. If seen by the death squads they are shot. Millions of children in the world are experiencing hell right now. There really is hell on earth.

Thinking of Calcutta's poverty I automatically think of Mother Teresa. Ever since I've been home people have told me how fortunate I was to have met her. Nobody, I can assure you, appreciates meeting this great human being more than me. Her home in the slums of Calcutta is the pinnacle of her work. I also think of all the other humanitarian work being done by thousands of ordinary people all over India - the unsung heros of poverty, outstanding social workers trying to improve the degrading poverty and misery around them. I know all the world has heard of Mother Teresa's work with the poorest of the poor in her home for the dying destitutes of Calcutta, and winning the Nobel Prize speaks volumes for her. But she would be the first to admit that she couldn't possibly have done any of it without the help of her very caring nuns and there are others working in Calcutta whose charitable work is just as important.

I now look back at a TV programme of more than 30 years ago, yes 30 years, and I can remember that particular programme quite vividly to this very day. It featured a truly remarkable Englishman. I can probably remember this programme so well because this man was someone very special indeed. Here was no ordinary man. He was loved by the poor of Calcutta. He was a giant of a man in every sense of the word, tall broad and upright with an enormous untrimmed beard. I would also like to mention here that he couldn't wear shoes because he was beaten mercilessly across the feet by the Japanese when he was a prisoner of war. I couldn't remember his name, though, until only quite recently when I picked up a book called Oxfam in Action. On flicking through its pages, there was a chapter on Calcutta. As I'm so fond of this impoverished city the book got my immediate attention. It mentoned the extraordinary work of Dudley Gardiner. If there are people to admire in this world, then this person would come near the top of my list. If he had been alive today I would have loved to have met him while in Calcutta.

Dudley Gardiner spent 32 years in the British army, mostly in India, as a private, Sergeant Major and officer. Here indeed was an officer and a gentleman. While in the army he devoted all his time to helping the under-privileged of India. On leaving the army, so committed was he to helping the poor that he stayed on in India and lived at the Salvation Army centre in Calcutta. He worked from dawn to dusk, helping the poor in any way he could, all voluntary work, of course. Just about all his army pension went on maintaining eight orphans, who he had picked up from the slums. The homes in these slums are known as Bustees. The orphans were put into boarding schools. He gave so much of his money and possessions away that he had little more than the dwellers of those appalling Bustees. On visiting the

Bustees he would care for the sick and bring them food. Some of the occupants looked as if they had stepped out of Belsen. Babies still continue to die there in shocking numbers. Cholera and tuberculosis are rife, along with countless other illnesses. Often the slum-dwellers are blind, crippled or paralysed. There are thousands of Bustees all over Calcutta. Every Bustee Dudley Gardiner visited he did his utmost to look after the inhabitants - it's a wonder he ever had time to go to bed at night, so occupied was he. Every evening he would drive his famous old truck round Calcutt's slums with hot soup and a slice of bread for all. At his nightly stops, hundreds of Calcutta's poor would be waiting for him. He did his best not to disappoint any of them. What a remarkable man he was. I can remember that TV programme so clearly, and on reading about him in that book I now have a clearer picture of him. This man was a hero to Calcutta's poor.

Dudley Gardiner must have died many years ago, but out of curiosity I looked for his name in the Chambers Biographical Dictionary of Famous Men and Women. This book listed 20,000 names spanning the centuries from the earliest times to the present day, Mother Teresa's among them. Included among the many famous names are judges, film stars, astronomers, prime ministers, bankers, sports stars, novelists and goodness knows who, but alas no Dudley Gardiner. Why not, I ask indignantly. I now realise I should have made inquiries about him while I was in Calcutta. But at that time I didn't know his name. I tell the story of Dudley Gardiner because he was just one among many others whose charitable work should never be forgotten. If Mother Teresa is rightly called the Angel of Calcutta, then Dudley Gardiner should have been its saint.

As Mother Teresa is the most famous person I'm ever likely to meet in my life, I did in fact carry out one of her wishes. While talking to her in Calcutta she had asked me to call on her sisters in the East End of London, so one day in July my wife and I called to see three sisters of her order who live and work in Stepney. The three we met were Sister Benicitta, Sister Simeon and Sister Innocentia. I felt I was with the Ursuline sisters again, and they had that same sense of humour. They are dedicated to their work with the poor in East London. They are out every day visiting the elderly and looking after children from broken homes. They even visit women in Holloway Prison once a week and they also feed the down-and-outs in Westminster every week until 1am. The hour-and-a-half my wife and I spent with them filled us with such admiration for their work. They also told us that they could be sent to any of the trouble spots of the world at any time. Fear is not a part of their lives. If God wants them, they are proud to serve him, wherever it may be. What wonderful women they are. Memories of the Divine Sisters of Tongo came flooding back. On leaving those three sisters in the East End of London I had the same feeling I had for the Ursuline sisters. It had been a privilege to meet them. They were so very pleased that I'd visited them. Mother Teresa had asked me to visit them and I was only too pleased to do exactly that.

Having been so fortunate to have met Mother Teresa I was naturally quite concerned when she had a suspected heart attack just before Christmas last year. She was taken ill in Mexico, just a few weeks after I had met her. and flown to a Californian hospital, where her condition caused great concern. When I was talking with her in Calcutta she mentioned how much she was looking forward to the visit of Princess Diana. Unfortunately, when Princess Diana visited Calcutta Mother Teresa was still in America. She was then transferred to a hospital in Rome, to where the very caring princess then flew finally to meet Mother Teresa in February of this year. Evidently, it was one of the Princess's dearest wishes to meet her. I understand the pair have become very close. Diana, with tears in her eyes, had said: "This meeting means so much to me." Having met Mother Teresa myself I knew exactly what she meant.

Sitting comfortably in my home right now, nine months after arriving home, I realise it was probably extremely foolish of me to walk completely on my own through those slums of Calcutta. I didn't just walk through the main streets of this city of millions, but I walked many miles through the backstreets as well. I was surrounded by thousands of Indians. Since I arrived home several people have asked me if I was frightened in any way. Apart from that one incident in the cemetery I was not. Somehow I trusted those people. But I realise now that I was putting myself in great danger. I could so easily have been mugged or killed. I rarely saw a white person in those two days I spent on my own in Calcutta. I could so easily have finished up missing along with countless others who just disappear every day in that city. I was taking a chance with my life, though I didn't realise it then. But sitting in the comfort of my own home I certainly do now.

Do you remember how infuriated I was when my camera was opened and the film destroyed by that security guard at Dum Dum Airport? The security at airports in India was, I thought, very strict indeed, perhaps too strict. Well, it really shook me rigid when just two days after I got home I was watching the 9 o'clock news and the newsreader said that a bomb had been found on the New Delhi to Gatwick 'plane just minutes before it took off. The flight was the very same one I had taken less than 48 hours previously. Well, if that bomb hadn't been found, all on board would have perished. Terrorism is now all part of the world we live in today. Security has to be strict at airports. Lockerbie proved that.

Any news of India in the papers or on TV will always get my immediate attention. Only recently Alan Whicker, on Whicker's World, was with a party of people on a tour of certain areas of the world. One particular programme focussed on the magnificent Taj Mahal. In his report Whicker said rain water carrying acids was causing severe damage to the very structure of the building. This acid rain was like a cancer starting to eat into the white marble and the Taj Mahal could begin to crumble. This incredible monument must be saved. India just cannot afford to lose an attraction which is a must for every visitor to the country. India is fast becoming a tourist country. Tourism brings money into India, which it can only benefit from. Alan Whicker said the Taj Mahal had lived up to his expectations. He said some monuments in the world hadn't quite lived up to expectations, but the Taj Mahal had. Having seen this monument of staggering beauty I couldn't agree more. It is aptly described as one of the Seven Wonders of the World. I only hope it stays that way.

Remember the day in Tongo when I was lying on my bed, hardly able to move because of the constant pain in my back, fearing what damage may have been done, and Sister Michael coming into my room saying that God had sent me to India on a mission? Well, I didn't take too much notice of what she said at the time, but you will recall I'd told Sister Bernadette that I would try to help in any way I could to repair that compound wall that circles the convent. I did mention in the introduction to this book that if it sells, then the proceeds would help to repair that wall. But I have to accept that my book may not sell, so I've had to rack my brains as to how I can raise the money any other way. It wasn't until May this year, however, that I hit upon an idea. Before I went to India the overseas officer of the local Inner Wheel club asked me if I would give a talk on my experiences at one of their meetings on my return. So, in May I spoke to about 50 members of the Inner Wheel club for about half an hour, and also showed them some of my slides. Afterwards I was presented with a cheque for £25 to put towards my chosen charity. I then decided to open a bank account in the name of Ursuline Convent School of Tongo. I have since spoken to other groups etc of My Indian Journey and I have come to the conclusion that if I give enough of these talks to organisations like Rotary clubs and Womens Institutes etc, it would be an ideal way of rasing money for the Tongo convent school wall. I've racked my brains as to how I could raise this £3,000. I hope that giving these talks is the answer.

I'm now in the process of sending dozens of letters out in the area where I live informing these different groups of my talks on India. The replies are coming in slowly and I've been very encouraged. People really are interested in My Indian Journey. I've probably got to do hundreds of talks to raise £3,000, but it is a start. It really did become an obsession with me while in Tongo to repair that wall and that obsession has not ceased since I arrived home. Sister Michael had told me that I'd been sent to India for a purpose - a mission, she called it. Well, if it's true I don't know of this. But what I do know is that if violence does come to the Tongo area, along with the Bihar thugs who go around terrorising people in other parts of the state, at least the sisters and schoolchildren will have some protection with the wall repaired. I can't bear to think of the consequences otherwise. I pray to God that violence never comes to Tongo.

So, as my reflections on India come to an end, what have I learnt personally? Seeing India was certainly an education. I've seen how some Indians live, or should I say survive. I know I shall never, for the rest of my life, forget the poverty I've seen. At times one had to see it to believe it. One thing I can say in all honesty is that I've got an awful lot to be thankful for, and that I do not take things for granted anymore. If I occasionally get depressed with work or life in general I immediately think of India, and my life is incomparable with that of literally millions of Indians out in the sub-continent. In fact, my advice to anybody is that if you're feeling sorry for yourself, go to a Third World country. I can assure you that you won't be sorry for yourself a minute longer. I now realise more than ever, not that I didn't before, that to be born in England and not India was my good fortune in life. I have a distinct advantage, a silver spoon if you like. The flick of a coin, and I came up trumps. But nearly a third of the world does not get the break I did when I was born. Millions of people in the world today are dying of malnutrition, but not me. I'm the lucky one, and I appreciate my life now more than ever. Life is precious, but to others in this world it's hell. Yes, whenever I get slightly depressed or sorry for myself I think of India. I can assure you, the reader, that the depression does not last for long.

I now come nearly to the end of my story. Sometimes I sit at home and I can't quite believe it has all happened. My wife has said that when I first arrived home on November 29 it was as though (and this went on for several weeks) my mind was still in India. I think that what I saw, and particularly the deprivation I'd seen, did have a deep, lasting effect on me and it took time to get back to a normal life again. It really was a momentous 22 days. I crammed more into those 22 days than into many a whole year of my life. I suppose that writing about My Indian Journey has also kept me very much involved. Every day since November 29 I have been writing this story. Perhaps when I've finished writing this book I can get back to normality.

In a way, writing this book has taken over my life, but I had to tell the story. Even if I do not get it published there will always be a record of it for my family and future generations. But my reason for writing this book, as I've already mentioned, is hopefully to sell a few copies of the published book so that the convent wall at Tongo can be re-built with cash from the proceeds. Another reason for my book is sponsorship in the Third World. I'm hoping that my story will inspire others to sponsor a child born into poverty. Thousands of children the world over are crying out for help. These children from the Third World need education. If they don't get it they will live an illiterate life just like their parents and forefathers. Once educated, these children's lives can only improve. I've seen sponsorship at work through Action Aid. Sponsorship brings happiness to these children. It gives them a chance in life. Albina Kujur had that chance and took it gratefully. She is just one from the whole sponsorship programme who has benefited from being sponsored. Believe me, it will also give the sponsor a lot of pleasure through helping a poor child somewhere in this world. Look at the pleasure I've had. All those letters I received from Albina over the years brought immense joy to me. If I'd never begun sponsoring a very poor girl from rural India, I would certainly never have met Albina. Need I say more?

Since arriving home I've received three letters from Albina, one within days. She was overjoyed that we had finally met. Of course, the whole purpose of my Indian trip was to meet her. What more can I say of her that's not already been said. She's desperate to pass those exams. She has something to prove in becoming a schoolteacher. She wants to earn her own living so very much. How fortunate I've been in meeting her. I travelled thousands of miles to rural India to do just that. It was a journey I'd always wanted to make. On reading that letter from Action Aid, which described those poor people's lives as an on-going cycle of misery from which they were unable to escape, I just had to find out for myself what life was really like there. Well, Albina's trying her best to escape. A poor girl from the tribe of Oron, from Mahatma Ghandi's India, is trying to carve out a new life for herself. But she will not forget her roots - the caste system won't allow it. And I've seen those roots, and from those roots I've met such a warm, friendly people. I'll remember that day spent with them at Albina's home forever. Yes, I'm the lucky one. I've met Albina. I've seen the Taj Mahal and the Eden Gardens cricket ground, and I've travelled through India - what more could any man ask for?

I'll close my Indian diary with the Divine Sisters of Tongo, those Brides of Christ who live at the Ursuline Convent School, Tongo. These sisters, along with all the other sisters throughout Bihar, are doing tremendous work for Indian schoolchildren. Some children just would not be getting an education if it weren't for them. The Divine Sisters of Tongo - and what an appropriate name it is for them - are my friends for life, these wonderful women who I'm so proud to have met. I can visualise all 16 of them sitting at that long table tucking into their rice at meal times, with very little light on and darkness outside. In one of her letters to me quite recently Sister Bernadette said that she always reads my letters to the others at the evening table. I can see their smiling faces right now, every one of them, their sense of humour which to me was such a lovely surprise. There is such laughter at the Tongo convent school.

When I left the Ursuline convent school at Tongo on November 27 to start my journey home I was close to tears as I said goodbye to all the sisters. Their warmth and affection to me was something I'll never forget. Their hospitality made my stay with them even more enjoyable than I'd dared hope for. As I've said previously in this book, I'd never stayed in a convent before - and to think I was going to stay in one in a foreign country, miles from anywhere and off the beaten track. One had to think what I was letting myself in for. But I realised quickly that any fears I had were completely unfounded. Yes, on saying goodbye I had a lump in my throat because, in all probability, I shall never see any of them again. Because of the life they've chosen, the sisters can be moved to other convents at any time. So if I were to visit Tongo again in later years a good half of the sisters could well have gone elsewhere.

Do you know that sometimes I can sit in the comfort of my own home, close my eyes and see a beautiful picture. I can see and hear the happy schoolchildren of Tongo singing, their voices flowing through those colourful, sloping forest hills of far away southern Bihar, that idyllic spot I found. If it weren't for the poverty it would be perfect. When those children sang it was as if those hills really were alive with the sound of music. When I was invited to the Ursuline convent school at Tongo I just didn't know what to expect. In fact, I didn't know what to expect wherever I was travelling during those 22 days. The travel brochures had said that in parts India was exotic, mystic, extremely colourful, wild and enigmatic. Yes, it was all that and much, much more. To me it was the trip of a lifetime. Memories to last forever. I wouldn't have missed My Indian Journey for anything. God bless India. I loved it.

India in Turmoil

It's now January 1993. I thought I had finished writing this book with Reflections, but certain happenings have prompted me to put pen to paper once again. India in Turmoil, the newspapers were saying in December last year, just over a year after I arrived home from that troubled country. At times India lives on a knife edge. Fighting between Muslims and Hindus can break out at any time. The latest disturbances came when Hindu fundamentalists attacked a long-disputed mosque in Ayodhya in northern India. This incident sparked off riots and bloodshed in many cities in the country. In Bombay alone more than 500 people were killed, terrible attrocities being carried out by both sides. To restore order Indian troops have been charged with mass rape and torture. More than 1,000 people have been killed in various parts of the country and are still being killed at time of writing. Even British Prime Minister John Major, on a visit to attend the country's 43rd anniversary celebrations, was not spared. Four Sikhs were arrested with remote controlled bombs which they intended to use on him. Other terrorist groups active throughout India were out to get him. Fortunately security was so tight at the Republic celebrations that he was not harmed. The biggest democracy in the world totters. Will it one day collapse? And yet in many respects it has been a model country for other developing nations. There has never been a coup d'etat. Democracy still rules in India, but only just.

Sister Bernadette Tete, in a letter received only a few days ago, spoke of the fear caused by this rioting. She described it as a difficult time. "All lived in fear and trembling. There is fear in everybody's heart and anything can happen at any time," she said. "No buses running and there is a curfew," she stated. I was hoping that Tongo, being well away from the big cities, would be reasonably safe, but not so, apparently. Sister Bernadette also wrote that vegetables, those so very precious vegetables that are grown in the convent garden, are being stolen every day. Burglars from the surrounding countryside and Tongo village itself are literally walking into the convent school grounds and helping themselves. At times the Ursuline sisters are too frightened to go out of the school grounds. If that's the situation, things are bad, very bad indeed.

Sister Bernadette also wrote that the convent wall was just as I left it. "If it's God's will then it will be repaired," she says. When I was staying at Tongo she was forever saying this. I've tried to imagine the present situation at the school. I shudder to think what could happen if the violence spreads to the country areas of India. The sisters and the schoolchildren at Tongo would be so very vulnerable with no protection at all. I once again realise the importance of getting that wall repaired. If real violence did come to their area the sisters would draw great comfort from God. He is their life. So many times during the day they are in the chapel for prayers. The Ursuline sisters are such gentle women. Violence is certainly not in their lives. If I was with them now they would be saying 'if it's God's will, what will happen will happen'. They genuinely accept this. Their faith in God has to be seen to be believed. I saw this faith while I was with them. They would give their lives to him. Their love for him is very real indeed. All I can say, having witnessed their love of God, is that they would certainly need him in times of crisis. But having said that, they would willingly lay down their lives for him.

The good news is that I've been accepted for the London Marathon on April 18, after four years of trying. You will recall that while I was staying at the convent school in Tongo I said that I couldn't possibly ask people back home to sponsor me for a marathon walk for a convent wall in India. Well, I've been proved wrong. People are only too pleased to help. If there are children involved, which there undoubtedly are, people respond in a positive way. The generosity of the Deepings, where I live, knows no bounds and continues to astound me. The plight of 1,300 schoolchildren in India has touched the hearts of many who I've asked to sponsor me. Also, the people who sponsor me will at least have the satisfaction of knowing that money collected by me will reach its proper destination - not like some money sent abroad, which often falls into the hands of unscrupulous people.

The bad news is that the £3,000 to repair the wall has now increased to £4,000, according to Sister Bernadette's latest estimate of the damage. I believe there is more damage than originally expected, so getting people to sponsor me for the London Marathon is another way of raising money to repair the wall.

I'm now in serious training for the London Marathon, which I shall walk and not run. I'm now gradually extending my morning walk, making it daily, and also beginning to extend the mileage. Sometimes my legs feel as though I'm picking up railway sleepers as I strive to beat the pain barrier. I'm not quite sweating blood, but it's tough going at times, a real hard slog. Sometimes I could walk all day. I feel like jumping out of my skin, so fit do I feel. Unfortuntely that feeling does not come along too often. But many a time my mind will drift to India and I will think of the slums of Calcutta. If my body aches I will think of those street kids once again. Whatever my pain, it is nothing in comparison to their's.

Their pain is a world without love and being thrown onto the streets to survive somehow. Survive for what, I ask. Surviving to a life of begging, thieving, scavenging, prostitution and early death - and to be spat at by the higher castes. And I think I've got problems. So after about 19 miles, when I could so easily pack it in, I shall shout to myself to stop whingeing. Those street kids of Calcutta will be in my thoughts and I can assure you my life will be put in its proper perspective. Yes, those street kids will keep me going during my London Marathon because whatever pain I might encounter it will be nothing by comparison to their pathetic lives.

Although India nearly brings me to tears at times. It has also brought me some absolutely hilarious moments, so if I'm seen laughing to myself on one of my long walks it could be that some amusing incident has got me chuckling to myself. What about that little man Misery at Agra. He was so very keen to fix me up with a woman. I shall never forget his peculiar look at my reply. The humour out in the streets of Calcutta I shan't forget either. I'll think of Sister Sushila rubbing oils into my back - those healing hands of her's - and how the sisters laughed while looking and probing at my back. Sister Vianney pouring the soup, need I say more? Sister Michael running after me in my haste to get to the toilet, with my trousers nearly down - what a picture that memory conjures up in the imagination - the Tongo schoolchildren on seeing my silly walk. How they howled with laughter. Falling into the river and being pulled out by Albina and Victoria. The sisters thought that was highly amusing. They could also see the funny side when Sister Angela failed to turn up for a date. There were so many amusing incidents at Tongo which even now continue to make me laugh. Yes, India brought me many memorable moments, some happy which I'll never forget, and some terribly sad moments that I shall remember to my dying day.

When I arrived home from India 14 months ago I put in my diary that I wanted to return. My ambition, therefore, is to go back one day, hopefully to see the Tongo convent school wall repaired. It may take one year or it may take five years to repair it, but I shall do it. Nearly 1,300 schoolchildren out in the sub-continent of India are relying on me to repair that wall. I can't let them down, can I?